Stock Market Profits

Seven Simple Secrets

Drew Sands

NorthStar Horizons, LLC

TABLE OF CONTENTS

LIST OF TABLES

Required Legal Notices

This book and the information provided herein is for educational purposes only, and no investment, tax, insurance, or legal advice is intended or given. The book is intended to provide general information on stock market trading. It does not purport to provide complete information on the stock market; nor is it intended to address specific requirements or to give specific instructions, either for an individual or an organization. The book is intended to be used as a general guide, and you are encouraged to read other books on the stock market and make your own judgments about what information best serves your individual needs

The author and publisher shall have no liability or responsibility to any person or entity and hereby disclaim all liability, including without limitation, liability for consequential damages regarding any claim, loss or damage that may be incurred, or alleged to have been incurred, directly or indirectly, arising out of the information provided in this book.

While the author has undertaken diligent efforts to ensure accuracy, there is no guarantee that this book contains no factual errors, omissions, or typographical errors. I believe that the data provided in this book are from sources that I deem to be reliable; however, I do not guarantee the accuracy or completeness of any such data. You should verify any such data through your own sources.

Nothing in this book should be construed to be (1) an offer to sell or a solicitation to purchase a security, or (2) a recommendation regarding any security. Information on specific securities used in examples is general in nature, is not tailored to the investment needs of any particular person, and should not be relied upon without independent verification.

Investing your money in the stock market is inherently risky. Your investment decisions are subject to certain risk factors that may not be discussed completely, or at all, in this book.

Your investment decisions and strategies should be determined solely by you, using your own judgment and taking into account any information provided to you by licensed professionals whom you may choose to consult, your unique investment objectives, and your personal financial circumstances. If you need professional advice, you should consult professional advisors of your own choosing.

This book may include information that is called "forward-looking statements" according to the Securities Litigation Reform Act of 1995. Forward-looking statements are inherently susceptible to uncertainty and changes in circumstances. That means that some of the statements in this book may be based on the author's assessment of things that might happen, as opposed to statements of fact about things that are already known to have occurred.

You can tell when you are reading a "forward-looking statement" because it will not be factually linked in a verifiable way to current or past actual events. Another indication to you of a forward-looking statement is seeing words such as "expect, plan, anticipate, hope, could, might, believe, estimate, predict, may, project, can, should, intent, is designed to, with the intent of, potential," and similar words or phrases that indicate that the author cannot tell you what the future will bring. However, the absence of such words does not necessarily mean that the statement is not forward-looking.

About the Author

Professional Background

Drew Sands has actively traded the stock market since 1967, when he completed his graduate degree at The American University in Washington, DC.

During his "real" career as a Personnel Research Psychologist with the U.S. Navy for 27 years, Drew conducted and directed dozens of research projects addressing the best recruiting, selection, and assignment strategies for both Navy enlisted personnel and commissioned officers, with a special interest in research design and quantitative analysis.

Over the course of that career, he published more than 60 book chapters, journal articles, and technical reports. In 1994, he retired from federal service as the Director of the Personnel Systems Research Department at the Navy Personnel Research and Development Center in San Diego, CA.

As a stock market consultant to both private individuals and businesses, he has custom designed, built, tested, and evaluated total stock trading systems for stock brokers, money managers, and private clients since 1991. Drew has taught in both academic and applied settings. In academia, he taught doctoral-level courses in advanced statistics and research design at the United States International University (now Alliant University) in San Diego, CA. Since 2002, he has also taught technical analysis and stock trading to VectorVest, Inc. customers/users in many cities across the United States.

Drew was the chief architect of the original VectorVest Technical Analysis course and taught it in seminars across the U.S. In addition to frequently being on the road teaching for VectorVest, Drew led the San Diego and Los Angeles VectorVest User Groups for five years.

He currently lives in Ocean City, Maryland, where he continues to be fascinated by the ever-changing stock market, and the ongoing challenges of identifying optimal trading strategies both for his consulting clients and for his own trading.

STOCK TRADING USER GROUP COMMENTS

"It is fun to watch your portfolio grow. Drew Sands' understanding of technical analysis indicators and the ability to teach their nuances made this happen."

Pam G., West Hills, CA

"The advice you gave me in understanding markets and investing generated a tremendous improvement to my investment returns."

Gus G., Los Angeles, CA

"As an active trader and teacher, Drew has done the extensive research required to help his students understand risk vs. rewards using various trading methods in any market situation. Once you understand Drew's time-tested principles, your trading results will greatly improve as mine have!"

Ed Alfaro, Aliso, CA

"I was immediately impressed with his organization, presentation skills and his in-depth understanding of technical indicators used in the trading of stocks and other financial instruments … I continue to marvel at his grasp of mathematical formulas as used in the art of Technical Analysis and the ease in which he can communicate this information to others. ... Drew is a natural leader, teacher, and conveyer of knowledge."

Chuck Castle, La Jolla, CA

"He is an excellent educator and researcher in the field of financial trading systems and a good source of valuable advice for those who wish to improve their trading skills."

Mark K., San Diego, CA

"Rarely will you find clarity, conciseness, and logical thought all from one investment teacher. That is exactly what you'll get from Drew Sands. He is an amazing and effective communicator. There are precious few rivals."

Doug G., Rancho Santa Margarita, CA

"Your expertise in the field of stock market technical analysis was clearly evident ..."

Dave Jadia, Los Angeles, CA

"I have worked with Drew for a number of years and we have worked together on trading projects using technical analysis techniques on numerous occasions. He is very conscientious when it comes to trading discipline and trading techniques especially when it comes to creating, testing and validating robust back-tested systems for trading."

Bill H., San Diego, CA

CONTACT INFORMATION

You can reach him by email:

StockMarketProfits@TradeByRules.com

WELL DESERVED THANKS

It has been my honor to work as a Technical Analysis Consultant and Senior Instructor for VectorVest since 2002. A large part of this book comes from my experiences with the company.

The VectorVest program was used to create the examples illustrating key points in this book. In addition, the money management approach employed is based upon selected *VectorVest Views* written by Dr. Bart DiLiddo, Founder and Chairman of the Board of Directors, VectorVest, Inc.

In addition to Dr. Bart DiLiddo, I am indebted to Mr. Don Payton, Chief Executive Officer, Mr. Mark Blake, Vice-President for Sales and Marketing, Mr. Steve Chappell, Director of Educational Services, and my fellow instructors for many valuable stock market insights and trading ideas.

Although Ms. Linda Royer, VectorVest Corporate Secretary/Treasurer, is not directly involved in the educational side of VectorVest, she has provided valuable policy guidance to me during my years with VectorVest.

In addition, I owe a debt of gratitude to my many consulting clients over the years and the thousands of students that I have had the privilege to teach. I have always believed in the philosophy behind the saying: "Sometimes a teacher, always a student."

I also want to express my appreciation to Chuck Castle who started and led the San Diego VectorVest User Group for years. Under his leadership, the group attracted many traders who used VectorVest products and others who found the user group presentations so valuable that they subscribed to VectorVest. Each user group

> "Anyone who stops learning is old, whether twenty or eighty. Anyone who keeps learning stays young. The greatest thing in life is to keep your mind young."
>
> -- Henry Ford

meeting involved stimulating presentations and lively discussions. I learned a lot about effectively using VectorVest from Chuck and these monthly meetings. In addition, I was able to contribute to the group by making presentations describing my research using VectorVest. Later, Chuck suggested to Dr. DiLiddo that I become the leader for the group and I served as the group leader for the next five years. Heartfelt thanks, Chuck, for all you taught me and for your vote of confidence!

Finally, I would like to thank my wonderful wife Margie for her encouragement and many contributions, which have substantially improved both the organization and readability of this book.

Any errors contained in this book are solely my responsibility. If you notice any errors, please notify me by email:

StockMarketProfits@TradeByRules.com

Ever Been Frustrated by the Stock Market?

"Sometimes we laugh, sometimes we cry,
but never do we throw our computers out the window."

Image Copyright Cartoonresource, 2013
Used under license from Shutterstock.com

Ever Been Frustrated by the Stock Market?

Stock market trading is a serious business, and stock market winners take a disciplined, business-like approach to their stock trading. Their approach includes the development and implementation of a trading plan that covers all the components of a complete stock market trading system.

In this book, I will teach you the crucial building blocks of exactly such a trading plan, starting with:

- Create your mission statement (you will likely lose money without one)

- Make a few essential decisions before you put one penny into the market

Then, to consistently make money in the stock market, you "only" need to:

- Minimize your risk of losing money in the stock market

- Get into the overall market at the best time

- Invest in the best business sectors and industry groups at the right time

- Identify stocks with a high profit potential

- Choose the best of those stocks to buy

- Buy your stocks at the best time

- Sell your stocks at the right time for maximum profit

But, get even one of these things wrong -- and you can quickly become one of those unhappy, frustrated traders who watches loss after loss pile up and then gives up, sadly concluding that you just can't be a successful trader.

I don't want that to happen to you! So, as you read this book, you will immediately see ways you can start getting all of these key issues right.

But wait ... there's more!!   To further help you make as much money as possible from your stock market trading, I will also show you how to:

- Keep trading records (you must do it - here is the best and easiest way)

- Maximize what you learn from <u>both</u> your profitable and losing trades

- Multiply your profits as you gain experience and knowledge from your trading records

Each and every one of these items is an absolutely essential "must-do" if you are looking for consistent, long-term trading profits. In this book, I will give you the information and guidance you need to create, implement, and maintain your own personalized stock market trading plan for consistently profitable trading.

WINNERS AND LOSERS

"*Normally I don't invest in tech stocks, but in this case...*"

WINNERS AND LOSERS

Like just about everything else in life, stock market traders include both winners and losers. And you want to be one of the winners, right? Congratulations! By purchasing this book, you have already completed a big step on your path to being a stock market winner!

Hi, I'm Drew Sands and I want to personally thank you for buying my book.

Over many years of stock trading, teaching technical analysis for the stock market to traders in many locations around the United States, designing and building total trading systems for dozens of clients, and leading various stock trading user groups, I have talked with thousands of stock traders.

In thinking back about those many discussions, I saw simple, dramatic, and clear-cut differences between the traders who made substantial profits from their trading activities and the traders who sadly watched their brokerage accounts suffer losses, trade after trade.

The vast majority of money-making traders shared a common core set of beliefs and practices. They had:

- Developed detailed, <u>written</u> trading plans;

- Consistently followed their trading plans;

- Maintained complete, detailed records of their trading activities;

- Periodically reviewed all their trades and goals;

- Regularly updated their trading plans to reflect changing market conditions, life circumstances, etc.; and,

- Continually learned from their trades and applied those lessons to their future trades.

In clear contrast, the traders who kept losing money had:

- No written trading plan (or, if they had a plan, they failed to follow their plan consistently);

- Made many trading decisions based on emotions, not rules;

- Kept minimal or no records of their trades; and,

- Apparently failed to learn significant lessons from their trading losses, repeating the same mistakes over and over again.

After thinking about these dramatic differences between the traders who consistently made profits and those who consistently lost money, I searched the internet and my own extensive library of trading books and magazines for a good reference that I could recommend to my consulting clients and students to help them create their own personalized trading plan.

To my surprise, I discovered that although many of the books and articles touched on some of the critical components of a good trading plan, none provided the detailed guidance that I think is essential. A trading plan should reflect your unique goals and trading style, and can pave the way for you to become one of those happy, successful traders reaping ongoing profits and a feeling of accomplishment and satisfaction from your trading.

Knowing the critical importance of a comprehensive written stock

> "The research is what I most enjoyed. It's like a treasure hunt doing research, because one discovery leads to another."
>
> -- Elizabeth Crook

market trading plan and discovering the lack of a good existing reference, I knew that I wanted to write this book. I think it will provide the guidance you need to create your own unique stock market trading plan and this, in turn, will lift your trading to a new level of profitability.

Trade by Rules,

Drew Sands

WHAT WINNERS DO

"It's better than beans, Jack. it's stock in the company that makes the magic beans."

What Winners Do

Trading Is A Business

In the earliest stages of starting any new business, a wise businessman will identify what he needs for his business, along with what assets he can invest into his business. As he starts his new business, perhaps his most valuable asset will be a thoughtful, comprehensive plan that includes goals for the new business and his strategy for meeting the initial startup costs and ongoing management requirements. The thoroughness and clarity of vision in his business plan will be one of the major (perhaps the major) determinants of whether this new business will be a success or a failure.

The same statement applies to your business plan for stock market trading. Unfortunately, many stock market traders do not really view their trading activities as a business. This is a serious error. Trading in the stock market should not be viewed as a gambling activity (Las Vegas would be better for that), nor should it be viewed as an opportunity to prove how smart you are (Mensa would be better for that).

> "By failing to prepare, you are preparing to fail."
> -- Benjamin Franklin

Your stock trading is a business, indeed a very serious business. Just like any other serious business, your trading should be guided by a comprehensive plan.

Estimates from various sources suggest that only about 10% of the people who attempt stock trading actually make money from their trading. Many, if not most, of the 90% of traders who lose money have made one or both of two critical errors:

- They did not invest the time to develop a thorough, written trading plan, or

- If they had a plan, they did not follow their plan and evaluate the results so they could improve their trading performance.

With so much at risk, why do so many intelligent, highly motivated people make such a serious mistake? Over the years, I have heard a variety of answers to that question.

Some traders argue that they don't have time to construct a good plan, or that the stock market changes so fast that any plan has very limited value. Of course, some of those traders manage to make some profitable trades even without a trading plan.

Unfortunately, this limited success just reinforces their belief that they do not need a trading plan. They fail to realize that their profits probably would have been substantially greater if they had developed and followed a sound, written trading plan, evaluated their results, and made changes to their trading based upon their evaluations.

Other traders, after failing to profit from their trading activities, realize that their trading activities have been inconsistent and not well thought out. Even worse, their trading losses have not taught them any lessons that they can use to make better trades in the future.

At this point, they either stop trading, concluding that trading "just isn't for them," or step back and begin to construct a written trading plan and a complete trading system. Of course, if they had done this to begin with, they would be working with more money in their brokerage account.

While having a written stock trading plan will not guarantee that you will make substantial amounts of money in the stock market, failing to make a written plan will substantially increase the probability that you will lose money. A mental trading plan is just not good enough to lead you to consistent and substantial trading profits.

Developing and following a detailed, written trading plan specifically designed for you

> "Sometimes, when people are under stress, they hate to think, and that's the time when they most need to think."
> -- Bill Clinton

as an individual trader will remove emotions from your trading and eliminate the two major causes of trading losses: fear and greed. The time you spend developing and maintaining your trading plan is an essential investment in yourself and your successful, long-term, consistently profitable stock trading.

You're Unique – Your Trading Plan Should Be Unique Too!

Every trader is a unique individual, and an effective stock trading plan should reflect that individuality. The dimensions below are some examples of the differences that call for substantially different trading plans and strategies.

Some traders have a large amount of risk capital to invest, while others trade a considerably smaller account size.

Some traders have a relatively long time horizon for their trades and trade infrequently, while others are more focused on short-term, high-frequency trading.

Some traders only pay attention to the stock market after the market closes, either because they have a full-time job other than trading, or they choose not to spend their days in front of their computer. Those traders only need end-of-day data. Other traders are active during the hours when the market is open, and those traders benefit from access to real-time data.

Some traders are conservative and emphasize preserving capital, while others are aggressive and focus on maximizing growth of their capital.

These different example dimensions, along with many others, result in a large number of different combinations that reflect different traders, account sizes, preferred strategies, goals, and risk tolerances.

Consequently, there is no "one-size-fits-all" trading plan. The only truly valuable stock trading plan for an individual trader is one designed for that trader.

BOOK OVERVIEW

My purpose in writing this book is to provide you with information and guidance for creating and maintaining your own individual stock market trading plan. My goal is for you to develop a plan that fits you as an individual, that you are comfortable with, that you will follow, and that will help you to achieve your stock trading objectives.

As you read the rest of this book, you will learn how to use the information on each of the following topics to maximize the money you are able to earn from trading:

- Mission Statement

- Battle Plan Preparation

- Money and Risk Management

- Stock Market Timing

- Business Sector and Industry Group Timing

- Stock Screening

- Stock Selection

- Stock Entries

- Stock Exits

- Trading Records

- Putting It All Together

You will find selected quotations throughout the book to help emphasize certain points. In addition, I have included some cartoons to inject a little humor into the serious business of stock market trading. I hope you enjoy them.

Ready to start doing what stock market <u>winners</u> do?

O.K. Let's get started!

Mission Statement

Mission Statement

Goals

The mission statement in your trading plan is your written description of the:

- Purpose and goals of your trading activities,

- Approach you intend to use to achieve your goals, and

- Ways you will evaluate your trading performance to monitor your progress over time and make changes as needed.

A mental picture of your mission is not likely to lead you to successful trading. In fact, many studies across various disciplines have shown that written goals are far more likely than mental goals to be pursued in a disciplined way and successfully achieved. Your goals should be clear, specific, and unambiguous. A vague mission statement like "My goal is become rich so I can quit my job" does not satisfy these criteria.

Approach

As you begin to consider the components of a trading plan to guide you to profitable trading, keep in mind that your approach to trading will be characterized by a number of inter-related dimensions.

Aggressive vs. Conservative

At the extremes, the aggressive trader is primarily concerned with capital appreciation, while the conservative trader is primarily concerned with capital preservation.

Using a baseball analogy, an aggressive trader is swinging for the home run, even though he expects to strike out frequently. A conservative trader is concentrating on hitting singles consistently, getting on base, and not striking out.

Everyone involved in stock trading should be concerned with both capital appreciation (maximizing profits) and capital preservation (minimizing losses). The issue for you, as an individual trader, is the relative importance or weight that you place on the two objectives to achieve a balance that is right for you.

Time Investment

Different traders are willing to spend different amounts of time working on their trading.

Day traders devote intense concentration to their trading during the stock trading day. A day trader typically enters and exits numerous stock positions during the course of each day. By definition, the day trader closes all positions before the market closes and, therefore, never holds a position overnight.

This appeals to people who enjoy the "action" of fast moving markets and frequent trading, while avoiding the risk of having open positions that can be adversely impacted by events occurring while the market is closed.

Swing traders hold positions for a few days or weeks, depending upon the performance of the stocks held.

Position traders or investors hold stocks over a longer period of time.

FUNDAMENTAL ANALYSIS VS. TECHNICAL ANALYSIS

Fundamental traders pay close attention to factors that influence the value of a stock, such as company management, earnings per share, earnings growth, competitive position of the company in its business sector, promising new products, etc.

Technical traders maintain that all the important information about a stock is reflected in the stock's price and volume. These two variables are often plotted on a chart for analysis of support, resistance, momentum, trends, and patterns.

TREND-FOLLOWING VS. CONTRA-TREND TRADING

Trend-following traders only enter positions when the stock has already demonstrated a trending pattern. This means, by definition, that the trader is not trying to catch the exact highs and lows of the stock prices, but rather is content to take profits from the middle of price moves.

Contra-trend traders, on the other hand, try to catch the peaks and valleys of a stock's price. They are attempting to capture the initial price movement that occurs just after a major reversal in trend, which can be substantial.

Novice traders are advised to adopt a trend-following strategy, at least in the initial phases of their stock market trading experience. Trend-following approaches are easier to implement, typically involve less stress and, many would argue, produce greater profits than contra-trend trading.

DISCRETIONARY TRADING VS. RULE-BASED TRADING

Discretionary trading involves looking at various factors that influence a trader to take a position in a stock, weighing these factors in a subjective way and implementing the trading decisions made using that informal consideration of market information.

In contrast, rule-based traders specify the exact rules of their trading strategy, including the rules for identifying advantageous market conditions, qualifing candidate stocks, choosing which stocks to actually trade, the money management rules for both the portfolio and individual stock positions, and the entry and exit rules for stock positions. Truly disciplined "rules" traders never enter trades that don't meet their rules exactly, no matter how promising a trade appears.

These objective, precise rules are frequently specified in a conditional "If X, then Y" formulation. For example, if the stock falls 10% from my entry price, I will exit immediately with an "at the market" sell order. The rules are so detailed and complete that the trader could give his rules to a neighbor, and that person could execute the trading strategy in exactly the same way that the trader himself would have acted.

I strongly believe that rule-based trading is by far the best approach to making significant amounts of money from your trading. First of all, trading by rules eliminates

> "Great things are not done by impulse, but by a series of small things brought together."
>
> -- Vincent Van Gogh

the trading mistakes that are so often based upon the emotions of fear and greed. In addition, this approach provides empirical evidence that you can use to document, scientifically evaluate, and improve a trading strategy.

PERFORMANCE EVALUATION METRICS

Your mission statement should clearly describe the measures that you will use to evaluate your trading strategy, including the measures you will use to describe profits and losses. Performance criteria are essential to understanding the effectiveness of your trading strategy and to making improvements. Specific performance evaluation criteria will be discussed in detail later in the *Trading Records* section of this book.

Here is an example of a good trading plan mission statement for a hypothetical trader.

Sample Mission Statement

My goal is to make 30% annual profit with a maximum drawdown of 15%. I will follow an aggressive trading approach, primarily based upon technical analysis. I will use a market timing system to identify the direction of the overall stock market. I will trade stocks using two strategies: a long strategy during up-market periods and a short strategy during down-market periods.

I will design and develop my own trading system that will be entirely rule-based, so that I can systematically backtest the system on historical data. Once my trading system satisfies my performance requirements in backtesting on historical data, I will paper-trade the system for at least 30 trades. If the system performs in a satisfactory manner (i.e., the system is on target to achieve my profit goals and is keeping losses controlled), I will begin trading it with real money.

My stock trading system will include the following seven key components:

- Market Timing

- Business Sector and Industry Group Timing

- Money and Risk Management

- Stock Screening

- Stock Selection

- Stock Entries

- Stock Exits

I will conduct my trading as a business and trade in a disciplined fashion, strictly following my system rules. I will document my trading performance for review, evaluation, and improvement. For every individual trade, I will record information on the entry, the exit, and the trade performance. I will maintain a cumulative record of my trades, including the number of trades, the total profits and losses, the rate of return, and the maximum portfolio drawdown.

I consider my trading plan to be a living document. Therefore, I will update my system rules as needed, based upon actual performance and lessons learned along the way.

Finally, I will continue to learn as much about stock trading as possible, through reading books and trading magazines, attending educational courses and trading conferences, and attending trading group meetings. I will be open to new trading ideas obtained from these sources and will rigorously backtest the promising ideas for possible future incorporation into my trading system.

Obviously, the sample trading plan presented above is a general example. Your individual trading plan will need to include specific details on the seven trading plan key components listed above (e.g., specific details on the market timing system and rules you plan to use).

SUCCESS STARTS HERE

"I need a list of specific unknown problems that we'll encounter."

Success Starts Here

Trading System

A complete trading system involves a number of component pieces which work together to produce your trading results. Each of these key components is discussed in separate sections of this book. These essential trading plan components include:

- Your trading approach (described in your mission statement),

- Money and risk management rules

- An overall stock market timing system

- A method for timing the broad business sectors and/or the specific industry groups of stocks

- A basis for screening stocks to identify qualified candidates

- A method of selecting the best stocks among the qualified candidates

- Stock entry procedures

- Stock exit procedures

You can buy an existing system and make your trades using the rules of that system; you can modify an existing system to reflect your trading situation and make your trades using the modified rules; you can develop a trading system from scratch; or, you can have someone develop a trading system for you.

Whatever the source of your trading system, it should be thoroughly backtested to assess its performance under a number of different stock market conditions. For example, a system might produce dramatic profits in a strong bull market, but using the same strategies in a level or declining market might result in substantial losses.

Backtesting is a procedure for simulating trades on historical data, tracking the trade results, and evaluating the effectiveness of the system. Many traders overlook this, or decide that it is too much work. They just identify a system that seems like a good idea, and begin trading that system with real money. This is usually a serious mistake.

After you are satisfied with how your system performs on historical data (backtesting), you should paper-trade your system using actual new stock market data with virtual money for at least 30 separate trades. This will give you additional evidence on the performance of your system on current market data. It will also give you practice with the mechanics of trading the system, without risking any actual money.

> "Never, **ever,** trade a system that has not been thoroughly backtested."
> -- Drew Sands

If you would like to explore having a custom-designed, total stock trading system developed, tested, and evaluated for you, please refer to the Consulting Services description at the end of this book for additional information.

BROKERAGE ACCOUNT

You must establish and fund a brokerage account to actually make trades. There are many brokerage houses competing for your business, and you should evaluate the major ones carefully by reviewing their features, costs, and reputations.

The brokerage account will supply the trading platform software. You will log into your account with the brokerage house, and use your brokerage company's software to actually make your trades, monitor your investments, and document your buying and selling activities.

If you are comfortable trading on your own, you can execute trades directly online. If, on the other hand, you would be more comfortable discussing your planned trades with a broker prior to implementing them, broker-assisted trading is usually available by telephone. This personalized assistance will increase your transaction costs, but may be a good investment for you.

INFORMATION COLLECTION

During the hours that the stock market is closed, you should review information provided by advisory services, the status of overseas market conditions, the futures markets, and news on the stock market as a whole and on individual stock companies.

During the first 30 to 60 minutes the stock market is open, you should monitor the status

> "If you think education is expensive, try ignorance."
> -- Derek Bok

of various stock market indices (e.g., the Dow-Jones Industrial Average, the Standard & Poor's 500 index, and the NASDAQ), for price changes, volume, and advance-decline statistics.

Frequently, the first 30 to 60 minutes of trading is marked by high turbulence, and is sometimes referred to as "amateur hour." After this initial period, price movements often tend to smooth out, be more gradual, and easier to trade because the risk of sudden, large price reversals is usually lower.

MONEY AND RISK MANAGEMENT

"Thanks for popping in at such short notice, I took the liberty
of inviting Ms. Stapleton.......our Grief Counselor

Image Copyright Cartoonresource, 2013
Used under license from Shutterstock.com

Money and Risk Management

Introduction

Money and risk management are crucial for a successful total trading system. Indeed, many authors maintain that money and risk management are the most important system components for successful trading. There certainly is no question that risk control is essential. If you lose all (or even a large portion) of your funds, you cannot continue trading.

Because investing in the stock market involves probabilities rather than certainties, losses are an inevitable part of stock trading, and reasonable losses should be considered as a cost of doing business.

For example, it is quite common for a trend-following strategy to only win about 35% of the trades taken. Even so, some of these trend-following strategies are quite profitable because the winning trades involve large dollar profits, while the losing trades are kept to small dollar losses.

Allocation of Funds

The first thing you should do is review your total financial picture (day-to-day living expenses, planned future expenses, emergency funds, vacations, investments, etc.).

Next, you should decide the amount of your investment capital that you want to place into stock market trading (vs. gold or silver, bonds, or other investments). You should view your stock funds as risk capital; i.e., money that would not have a serious adverse impact on your style of living if you lost it.

Let me say that again: **You should not be trading with any money that you cannot afford to lose.**

Many people have two accounts and use a different trading system for each account. Often, they have a conservative account that contains the major portion of their stock trading funds and an aggressive account containing a smaller amount.

If your plan involves two trading accounts (one aggressive and the other conservative), you need to allocate your total stock trading funds between the different accounts and use a different trading strategy for each account. Aggressive trading strategies are quite different from conservative strategies.

TYPES OF RISK

As you plan and manage your stock trading, you need to be aware of some risk factors that you face as a trader. In addition to the various general types of risk that can affect any financial asset (e.g., inflation, interest rates, etc.), two more specific types of risk deserve special attention for stock trading: Portfolio Risk and Stock Risk.

Portfolio Risk

The issue of portfolio risk addresses the question: How much of your trading account can you afford to put at risk?

Suppose, for example, you start with $100,000 in your account and lose 10% of it on your first trade. Your account balance is now $90,000. To get back to even, you need to make a profit of $10,000.

Without thinking it through, some people might say that since they lost 10% on their first trade, they need to make 10% to recover. Not true!

You will be making your new trade(s) based upon a decreased account balance of only $90,000, so you actually need to make a profit of 11.1% just to boost your account balance back up to $100,000.

Suppose you lost 50% from your original account balance of $100,000. You would need to make a profit of $50,000 to recover (i.e., a percent gain of 100%). While this example is easy to see, the percent required to recover from other percent losses is more difficult to determine without a formula.

Equation {1} provides the formula for calculating the percent gain required to recover from a specified percent loss.

$$\{1\} \ PR = 100 * [1 / (\{1 / (PL / 100)\} - 1)]$$

where:

PR is the percent required to recover from a given percent loss and,

PL is the percent loss.

Using the first example discussed above (10% loss) to illustrate the application of Equation {1}:

$$PR = 100 * [1 / (\{1 / (10 / 100)\} - 1)]$$
$$= 100 * [1 / (\{1 / (0.1)\} - 1)]$$
$$= 100 * [1 / (\{10\} - 1)]$$
$$= 100 * [1 / (9)]$$
$$= 100 * [0.111]$$
$$= 11.1$$

For your convenience, Table 1 shows the percent gain required to recover from various percent losses ranging from 1% to 99%. Please take note of how suddenly the percent profit you would need to recover from your losses rises to very high profit goals that are unlikely to be achieved. You can see that keeping your losses under control is essential to the success of your trading.

Table 1: Percent Gain Required To Recover From Various Percent Drawdowns

Percent Drawdown	Percent Gain To Recover	Percent Drawdown	Percent Gain To Recover
1	1.01	55	122.22
5	5.26	60	150.00
10	11.11	65	185.71
15	17.65	70	233.33
20	25.00	75	300.00
25	33.33	80	400.00
30	42.86	85	566.67
35	53.85	90	900.00
40	66.67	95	1900.00
45	81.82	99	9900.00
50	100.00	100	~

Particularly, note that the relationship between the percent drawdown and the percent gain required for recovery shown in Table 1 is markedly nonlinear, especially at the upper end. Relatively small differences in the drawdown result in very large differences in the gains required to recover from the loss.

A maximum portfolio drawdown goal of 15% is acceptable to many traders. A 15% loss would require the trader to make 17.65% profit to recover from the loss, a level of performance which is a reasonable goal.

Now, let's look at a somewhat larger example of loss. It is extremely dangerous to allow your losses to exceed 25% of your account size. Recovery from a 25% drawdown will require you to make 33.33% profit on your remaining money (a feat that is challenging to achieve) just to replace your losses.

If you allow your losses to reach 50%, you will have to double your money before you reach the breakeven point, a challenge that few traders will be able to accomplish. Again, you can easily see why it is so important that you carefully manage this aspect of your trading activities.

Stock Risk

What percent of your trading account can you afford to risk in a single stock position?

First, it should be noted that your "affordable risk" amount is not the same as the total amount of money invested in an individual stock.

Assuming you are using stop-losses, the amount of risk for an individual stock position is the difference between your entry price and your stop-loss exit price.

You should be protecting yourself with stop-loss orders on all your open positions to limit your losses. Stop-loss orders will be discussed in the *Stock Exits* section of this book.

Dr. Bart DiLiddo wrote about managing the percent risk for an individual stock position in the February 6, 2009 edition of the *VectorVest Views*. He presented a method to determine this risk as a function of the percent of your overall portfolio capital invested, the number of stocks in your portfolio, and the stop-loss you use. He provided the following formula for calculating the percent risk on a single stock position:

$$\{2\}\ R = (C / N) * (S / 100)$$

where:

> R is the percent risk for a single stock position;
>
> C is the percent of the portfolio capital employed;
>
> N is the number of different stock positions; and,
>
> S is the stop-loss percent used.

To illustrate, suppose you decided to use half of your total funds to open five stock positions and that you planned to use a 10% stop-loss order for each position. Substituting this information into the formula:

$$R = (50 / 5) * (10 / 100)$$
$$= (10) * (0.1)$$
$$= 1\%$$

You would be risking 1% for each individual stock position.

If you wanted additional diversification and expanded the number of stocks in your portfolio from five to ten, while keeping the other factors the same, you would reduce the percent risk for an individual stock by half, as shown in the following example:

$$R = (50 / 10) * (10 / 100)$$
$$= (5) * (0.1)$$
$$= 0.5\ \%$$

Finally, suppose you wanted to invest all your portfolio funds into ten stocks, and still planned on using a 10% stop-loss level for each stock:

$$R = (100 / 10) * (10 / 100)$$
$$= (10) * (0.1)$$
$$= 1\%$$

From these examples, you can begin to see the interaction between the factors. Obviously, there are various ways to satisfy your risk objective.

STOCK MARKET TIMING

"And in the event of a sudden drop in the market, oxygen masks will drop from above your seats."

Stock Market Timing

Introduction

Market timing is one of the most important factors in an effective, profitable, total stock market trading system. Many people start out spending a lot of their time on individual stocks, and then give only passing consideration to what the market as a whole is doing. That is usually a bad allocation of your planning time.

A more effective approach is to look at your trading from a top-down perspective, wherein you first consider the stock market as a whole (e.g., the S&P-500), then consider the broad business sectors (e.g. computers), then more narrowly defined industry groups within the business sector (e.g., computer printers), and finally the individual stock (e.g., Dell Computer).

While it is possible to buy an individual stock and make a profit even though the market, the business sector, and the industry group are all falling in price, your odds are not favorable. Your probability of making money is greater if you trade in the direction that the overall market, broad business sector, and specific industry group are moving; i.e., trading with the wind at your back.

Market Forecasting vs. Market Timing

Market forecasters use various economic factors to predict what the stock market will do in the future. Some of these market forecasters have been successful in their predictions and have developed a following of stock market participants anxious to know where to put their money in advance of market moves. Unfortunately, even the best of the market forecasters eventually make an erroneous forecast.

Market timers, on the other hand, wait for the stock market to tell them what it is doing and

> "Forecasting is very difficult, especially if it's about the future."
>
> -- Niels Bohr

then they jump on board for the profit ride. While the actionable signal generated by market timing is somewhat later than a market forecast, this approach has a higher probability of being profitable.

There are two approaches to using market timing in your trading decisions: technical analysis and calendar patterns. These approaches are not mutually exclusive and may be used in combination.

MARKET TIMING BASED ON TECHNICAL ANALYSIS

Many market timing strategies for stock trading employ one or more technical analysis indicators to signal periods when the market is likely to rise or fall. These technical analysis indicators, which can be somewhat complex, are really based on only two pieces of information: price and volume. Even so, traders can choose from hundreds of technical analysis indicators available in the literature (a testimony to creativity!).

While including many different technical analysis indicators in a trading system may appear to enhance accurate decision-making, the information you get will be largely redundant. This can lead to unwarranted confidence in your conclusions. In addition, the more indicators you are using, the more possibility there is for conflicting guidance from the indicator set. This can easily lead to "analysis paralysis," and make it difficult to take action.

To deal with this, I suggest that you use a maximum of five technical analysis indicators, making sure to include some based upon price and others based on volume. Many traders are quite successful using fewer than five indicators.

> "We are drowning in information but starved for knowledge."
> -- John Naisbitt

MARKET TIMING BASED ON CALENDAR PATTERNS

In addition to mathematical systems, there are also many calendar-based market timing systems. These systems identify periods during which it is usually advantageous to be in the market, and periods during the year when it is better to be on the sidelines in a cash position.

A good example of this type of market timing system is described by Jeffrey A. Hirsch and J. Taylor Brown in *The Almanac Investor: Profit From Market History and Seasonal Trends*. They describe a system called the "Best Six Months Switching Strategy" that invests in the Dow Jones Industrial Average from November 1 until April 30. Traders following this system switch into fixed income approaches from May 1 until November comes again. Overall, this strategy has been quite successful since 1950.

CONCLUSION

Any long trading strategy (buying a stock anticipating that its price will rise) except a "buy and hold" approach will, by definition, involve periods of time when there are active trades open, and other periods where the trader is on the sidelines with no active stock positions.

This trading approach will require some basis for determining when to have long, bullish stock positions and when to be in cash with no open positions. Aggressive traders who want to make money in both up and down markets will also need rules for determining when to have open short, bearish positions (selling a stock that you have borrowed from your broker, anticipating its price will fall, and then actually buying the stock later and, hopefully, at a lower price to return to your broker).

If you choose not to use a "buy and hold" strategy, you can adopt one of the numerous market timing systems available in the literature, modify an existing system, design and develop a new system, or have a custom system

> "They also serve who only stand and wait."
>
> -- John Milton

developed for you. Regardless of the choice, your market timing system should be thoroughly tested and evaluated before incorporating it into your trading system and using it to trade actual funds.

If you do not feel that you have the knowledge to backtest your system properly, then you should get someone with the necessary expertise and experience to design, analyze, and evaluate your system before you make any trades with it.

If you would like to explore having a custom-designed, total stock trading system developed, tested, and evaluated for you, please refer to the Consulting Services section at the end of this book for additional information.

Business Sector & Industry Group Timing

"Sell all our mining and Resources stocks, NOW!"

Image Copyright Cartoonresource, 2013
Used under license from Shutterstock.com

BUSINESS SECTOR & INDUSTRY GROUP TIMING

DESCRIPTION

The examples in this section were developed using the VectorVest program. As mentioned in the previous section, I think that trading stocks should follow a top-down approach:

- Overall stock market (e.g., S&P-500)

- Broad-based business sectors (e.g., Food)

- More narrowly defined industry groups (e.g., Candy); and, finally

- Individual stocks (e.g., Hershey Foods)

Various providers of stock market data have organized individual stocks into their own industry groups and business sectors. For example, VectorVest provides data on 7939 individual stocks (as of May 24, 2013). These stocks are categorized into 220 Industry Groups which, in turn, are grouped into 41 Business Sectors.

When the VectorVest program displays either Industry Groups or Business Sectors, they are rank-ordered from high to low based upon relative timing, an index that describes the average price momentum. Using an example from VectorVest (May 24, 2013), the Computer business sector contained seven industry groups, rank-ordered by relative timing from highest to lowest:

- Memory Devices

- Peripheral Equipment

- Graphics

- Makers

- Systems

- Networks

- Services

The Computer Makers industry group (the fourth group listed above), for example, included the following eight stocks (as of May 24, 2013), rank-ordered from high to low by the VectorVest Composite, a proprietary index used to characterize a stock based upon its value, safety, and timing:

- Apple Inc (APPL)

- Silicon Graphics International (SGI)

- Lenovo Group (LNVGY)

- Hewlett-Packard Co. (HPQ)

- Cray Inc (CRAY)

- Dell Computer (DELL)

- Steel Cloud Inc (SCLD)

- Super Micro Computers Inc (SMCI)

When you can identify a strong, up-trending stock that is part of an up-trending industry group in an up-trending business sector and the overall market is also moving up, you have a situation with very good profit potential. This is an example of trading with the wind at your back.

<u>EXAMPLE</u>

Many people who adhere to the top-down approach will first look at

> "One of the soundest rules I try to remember when making forecasts in the field of economics is that whatever is to happen is happening already."
> -- Sylvia Porter

market timing and then consider either business sectors or industry groups (but not both) as the next tier, before evaluating individual stocks. My preference between the two is industry groups, as they provide a more focused picture than the broader business sectors.

Suppose that the particular market timing strategy you use is giving an "Up Market" signal. At this point, you could determine which industry groups are rising the fastest and then consider the stocks in those industry groups as qualified candidates.

In VectorVest, you can build a search to identify stocks belonging to the industry groups that are rising the fastest on average. A search conducted on May 24, 2013 produced 75 candidates that belonged to the following top five industry groups, based on relative timing:

- Retail (Department Stores)   10 stocks

- Aerospace & Defense (Elec)   3 stocks

- ETFs (Sector\Biotech)   6 ETFs

- Electrical (Connectors)   6 stocks

- Retail (Apparel)   50 stocks

By following your market timing strategy and focusing on the stocks and ETFs in these five industry groups, you would have both market timing and industry group momentum on your side.

STOCK SCREENING

"All my success is based on good decisions. All my failures are somebody else's fault."

STOCK SCREENING

DESCRIPTION

The stock screening component of trading involves specifying a set of criteria for:

- Identifying stocks that are qualified candidates for selection, and

- Screening out those stocks that do not meet all of the various qualification criteria.

These screening standards will differ for each trader depending upon a variety of individual factors (e.g., risk tolerance).

EXAMPLES

As you make a single screening criterion more and more stringent, fewer and fewer stocks will be considered "qualified" for selection. Again using the VectorVest stock database (January 20, 2012) to demonstrate, let's examine the consequences of requiring the current stock price to be greater than various minimum criterion levels.

Table 2: Number of Qualified Stocks Decreases As Minimum Price Criterion Increases

Minimum Stock Price Criterion	Number of Qualified Stocks
Price > $0.00 (Entire Database)	8379
Price > $5.00	5618
Price > $10.00	4625
Price > $15.00	3643
Price > $20.00	2901
Price > $25.00	2405
Price > $50.00	947
Price > $75.00	373
Price > $100.00	196
Price > $200.00	77
Price > $500.00	38
Price > $1,000.00	17

As you can see, setting the minimum stock price to greater than $5.00 reduces the number of stocks considered qualified from the 8379 stocks in the entire database to 5618 stocks. As the minimum price criterion continues to be raised, the number of stocks considered to be "qualified" candidates continues to decrease.

As another example, suppose you only wanted to consider stocks belonging to the S&P-500. You can set up a search in VectorVest to include only the S&P-500 stocks, and screen out all others. Such a search would, of course, yield only the 500 stocks that are included in the S&P-500 Index.

You can see that adding just a single stock requirement (for example, minimum price or membership in the S&P-500 Index) dramatically reduces the number of stocks that you will be considering. Now imagine what happens when you require that selected stocks must meet two or more requirements.

For each different criterion that you add to the search, the number of stocks that meet **all** the qualifications decreases, as shown in Table 3.

Table 3: Number Of Qualified Stocks Decreases As Additional Screening Criteria Are Added

Cumulative Screening Criteria	Decreasing Number of Qualified Stocks
None (Entire Database)	8379
S&P 500	500
Price > $25.00	389
Average Daily Volume > 2,000,000	232
Dividend Paid > $2.00	19

In this example, only 19 of the 8379 stocks in the VectorVest database met **all** the above requirements. If you continue to include additional criteria, eventually there will be a point where no stocks will meet all the criteria.

STOCK SELECTION

Image Copyright Cartoonresource, 2013
Used under license from Shutterstock.com

STOCK SELECTION

RANK-ORDERING QUALIFIED CANDIDATES

The stock screening process described in the previous section eliminates all those stocks not considered to be qualified candidates because they failed to meet one or more of the qualification rules. Even so, the resulting list of viable investment candidates could potentially include hundreds or even thousands of stocks, depending upon the number of screening standards and the stringency of those criteria. Obviously, you do not (or should not) want to open positions in all these "qualified candidates."

Therefore, you need some basis for rank-ordering the qualified stocks from most to least desirable for actual trading. One approach is to identify the most important characteristic of qualified stocks and rank-order the list from best to worst on that variable. For example, stocks could be rank-ordered from high to low based upon the percent price change in the previous day or the previous week.

A variation on this approach would be to combine multiple key dimensions into a composite score for each stock (i.e., a single number that describes the overall potential of each stock). This composite score can be used to rank-order your qualified candidate stocks and enable you to pick the top ones for actual trading.

VectorVest, for example, rank-orders stocks based upon the VectorVest Composite (VST) score for each stock. This VST score is based upon a combination of a stock's Relative Value score (RV), Relative Safety score (RS), and Relative Timing score (RT).

The Relative Value score represents a stock's price appreciation potential over the next three years. The Relative Safety score assesses the predictability and consistency of the stock's financial performance. The Relative Timing score is a measure of a stock's price trend momentum.

BEST NUMBER OF STOCKS FOR YOUR PORTFOLIO

The total dollars you have available for trading should influence your decision on the best number of stocks to include in your portfolio. Obviously, if you have a million dollars in your account, you should include more different stocks in your portfolio than if you have five thousand dollars in your account. Another consideration affecting the "best" number of stocks to include in your portfolio is your risk tolerance and your position on the aggressive – conservative continuum.

Theoretically, the single best stock is at the top of the rank-ordered list produced by the process described in the previous section. The most extreme aggressive approach would be to invest all your assets into this one best stock.

However, this approach provides no diversification and is the epitome of "having all your eggs in one basket." On the other extreme, if you divide your total account assets among the top 50 qualified candidate stocks, you will achieve a highly diversified portfolio.

Note, however, that while the payoff from diversification initially rises with the addition of stocks to the portfolio, it begins to have diminishing incremental value as more and more stocks are added to the portfolio.

Furthermore, having a portfolio of 50 stocks will involve 50 entry and 50 exit transaction costs, which will create a substantial cost to overcome before portfolio profits are achieved. Finally, the day-to-day monitoring and management of 50 stocks would be extremely time-consuming.

Considering all of the above variables, I think that a good starting number of stocks for many traders is ten, with a reasonable range being between 5 and 15.

EXAMPLE

Let's suppose that we want to have ten stocks in our portfolio. Using the most stringent search described in the previous section, there are 19 stocks that are qualified candidates for inclusion in our portfolio as of Friday, January 20, 2012.

How would we rank-order the 19 qualified candidate stocks so that we can select the best ten to enter on the next trading day (Monday, January 23, 2012)? In VectorVest, this task is accomplished by using the sort variable.

If we wanted to buy the ten stocks that rose the most during the most recent trading day (January 20, 2012), we would use the percent gain to sort and rank-order the 19 qualified stocks from high to low and select the top 10.

While all 19 stocks met all of our qualification standards, we would plan on entering these top 10 stocks on January 23, 2012 with an equal-dollar amount used for each of the ten positions (assuming that our market timing system was signaling "Up Market").

Table 4: Rank-Ordered Qualified Candidate Stocks

Rank	Company	Symbol	% Gain
1	Int'lBusMach	IBM	4.43
2	Century Tel	CTL	1.28
3	Phillip Morris	PM	1.00
4	FirstEnergy	FE	0.95
5	NextEra	NEE	0.88
6	Union Pacific	UNP	0.59
7	PepsiCo Inc	PEP	0.56
8	Equity ResPty	EQR	0.47
9	McDonalds	MCD	0.47
10	Proctor & Gmbl	PG	0.23

Stock Entries

"What do you see in emerging markets?"

Stock Entries

Introduction

The topic of stock entries is a popular one for stock traders and always receives considerable attention. A review of the presentation titles at a trading conference (e.g., the Money Show or the Traders Expo) will reveal a host of presentations related to stock entries and comparatively few presentations related to stock exits.

Apparently, many, if not most, traders think that issues involving stock entries have the biggest impact upon their trading success. If you are one of these people, you may be very surprised by my discussion of stock exits in the next section (*Stock Exits*).

Timeframe for Stock Entries

The timeframe for stock entries is an important consideration in your total stock trading plan. For example, if you have a full-time job that prevents you from watching the market during the trading day (or you choose not to), you will need to make your investment decisions and place your order with your on-line broker the night before the planned entry day or before the market opens.

On the other hand, if you can (and want to) watch the market as it opens on the day you wish to enter stock positions, you have an advantage because you can observe the overall market conditions during the first part of the trading day and then decide if this will be a day that is favorable for you making a profit. If market conditions do not look good, you can elect to not trade that day and wait for a better opportunity.

ENTRY STRATEGIES

All-In

In this type of entry strategy, the entire position in each target stock is filled at once. This will have the advantage of a single transaction cost. If the price moves up in accordance with your plan, you have established all of your stock positions at a relatively low entry price.

Scaling-In

In this type of entry strategy, the total desired number of shares in a stock is purchased in two or more stages, assuming the price moves in your direction after each stage. This approach has the obvious drawback of multiple transaction costs.

In addition, the total per-share entry cost will be greater than the entry cost of the "all-in" approach, because you will have paid more for the stock in the second stage of your purchase than you paid for the same stock in the initial stage.

On the other hand, if the stock price moves against you after the initial purchase, you do not follow with a second stage purchase and, therefore, you lose less than if you had purchased the full number of shares initially.

ORDER TYPES

Four types of orders are frequently used to enter stocks:

Market Order

This order is executed immediately at the current market price. Execution of the order is guaranteed but not the purchase price. In my opinion, a market order is more appropriate for an exit order than an entry order. When your trading system signals an exit (e.g., a market-down signal), you want to get out as soon as possible. When you are entering positions, there is not as much urgency.

Finally, I do not think that a market order should be entered when the market is closed because the order will be executed at the next opening of the market, and your stock purchase price may be substantially different from what you expect.

Limit Order

This order is executed at a specific price or better. While your price is guaranteed, the execution is not. This type of order prevents unpleasant surprises about execution prices. On the other hand, the order may, or may not, be filled. The drawback of using a limit order is you may miss getting into a stock that never quite reaches your limit price and starts rising rapidly.

Stop Order

Once the buy stop price is reached, this order becomes a market order and is executed immediately at the current market price.

Stop-Limit Order

This order combines a stop order with a limit order. Once the stop price is reached, the order becomes a limit order that will be executed at the limit price or better.

While there are other types of orders, these are the most frequently used order types.

Stock Exits

Image Copyright Cartoonresource, 2013
Used under license from Shutterstock.com

Stock Exits

Importance

As previously mentioned, a review of the agenda for trading conferences (e.g., the Money Show or Traders Expo) will reveal that many of the presentation topics focus on stock selection and entries.

Since speakers attempt to lure as many people as possible to hear their presentations, one can infer that they believe that entry strategies are what the attendees want to learn about and relatively little attention is given to exit strategies.

You may be surprised to learn that, despite the fact that most people focus on strategies for entering stock positions, the strategies employed to exit stock positions are far more important for your trading profits.

When the topic of stock exits comes up, one of the golden rules for trading that you will hear frequently is: "Let your profits run and cut your losses short." This rule is easy for people to understand, yet is very difficult for many traders to actually follow. Why is this seemingly simple strategy so difficult to carry out?

Actually, there are two reasons behind this difficulty – both of them rooted in basic human nature.

Let's start with the profits part. When you buy a stock and the price starts rising, you get a positive feeling for two reasons. Obviously, making a profit is viewed positively. In addition, the profit provides positive reinforcement on your investment decision. Everyone likes to be right about their decisions.

If the stock price begins to fall back and the profit begins to disappear, you may be panicked into selling the position to prevent the profit from turning into a loss, thus protecting both your funds and your ego.

Many traders use a trend-following strategy to decide the timing for entering their stock positions. Typically, a trend-following strategy will have more losing trades than winning trades.

Despite this relatively low winning percentage, trend-following is popular because the average dollar amount of the wins is usually far larger than the average dollar amount of the losses. This may seem like a simple point, but its implications are crucially important to understand and to implement.

When you have many losing trades and only a few winning trades, you must take advantage of the large potential gain for each and every one of those winning trades.

If you exit as soon as your profit starts to decrease, you eliminate the opportunity for larger gains, a key component of a winning trend-following strategy.

Now let's look at the second part of that golden rule which advises the trader to cut losses short. When a trade is entered and the

> "Self-discipline is an act of cultivation. It requires you to connect today's actions to tomorrow's results. There's a season for sowing, a season for reaping. Self-discipline helps you know which is which."
>
> -- Gary Ryan Blair

price starts moving downwards producing a loss situation, many traders will be reluctant to admit that they have made a poor decision.

They rationalize that they have done adequate research and that their original opinion was correct. They believe that the stock marketplace is wrong, and that the price will turn around and begin rising.

When the price continues to fall, they still may be unwilling to exit their position and admit their mistake. Sometimes, they will change their original profit goal and plan to exit if the price will just rise back up to their breakeven point. Their ego is still interfering with sound judgment.

If the price continues to fall, most people will eventually give up and exit their losing position. At this point, they are taking a big loss, instead of the small loss they could have taken if they had closed their position earlier.

Keep in mind that virtually every large loss starts out as a smaller loss. Now it becomes clearer why this golden rule seems to be difficult to follow for many people.

The book *Technical Traders Guide to Computer Analysis of the Futures Market* by Charles LeBeau and David W. Lucas (1992) contains some of the best research I have ever seen on exits, and the book is widely respected by trading professionals.

In his excellent book, *Trade Your Way to Financial Freedom* (1999), Van K. Tharp credits Chuck LeBeau with drawing a strong connection between this golden rule of trading and the importance of exits.

Tharp notes that both the profit and the loss portions of the golden rule concern exits. He cites a study by Tom Basso, who designed and conducted research to demonstrate the relatively large importance of exit and money management strategies, compared to the relatively small importance of entry strategies (Tharp, p. 200).

Tom Basso conducted his study to address the following question: Can a trading system produce consistent profits with a random entry strategy, coupled with a sound money management strategy and exit strategy?

He tested his system of position-sizing and exits using a random ("coin-flip") entry strategy on four different futures markets. The system was always in the market (long or short, based upon the "coin-flip").

Once an exit signal was generated and executed, the market was re-entered immediately, based upon the random signal. Results showed a consistent profit, even allowing $100 per trade for commission and slippage.

Tharp investigated Basso's approach on ten additional markets. Tharp's system included the following components:

- Entry – random trade direction (either long or short);

- Money Management – a 1%-risk position-sizing strategy;

- Exit – a trailing stop based upon a volatility measure, calculated as three times the 10-day exponential average of the average true range (a technical analysis indicator).

Since the study included a random entry signal, the results differed somewhat across simulation runs. When only one futures contract was traded, the system made money 80% of the time. When a 1%-risk position-sizing strategy was added to the system, it was profitable 100% of the time.

Recalling that the direction for each position (long or short) was randomly determined in these two studies, the results underscore the critical importance of money management and exit strategies and the relatively smaller importance of the entry strategy.

EXIT STRATEGIES

All-Out

In this type of exit strategy, the entire open position in a stock is closed at once. This has the advantage of a single transaction cost. If the position is losing money, this will stop the losses immediately. If the position is making money, this will lock in the profit. However, if the price continues to improve, the additional profit will not be realized.

Scaling-Out

In this type of exit strategy, the entire open position in a stock is closed in two or more stages. This will involve the disadvantage of multiple transaction costs. If the position is losing money, this strategy will lose more money than an all-out strategy would lose (assuming the price continues the losing trend). However, if the price is improving and continues to improve, this strategy will capture the additional profit because the second exit will occur at a more favorable price than the initial exit price.

PROFIT-BASED EXITS

Planned exits for profitable stock positions can take a variety of forms. For example, the trader can establish a profit objective at the outset of the trade. This could be based upon a certain dollar amount or, more typically, a specified percentage gain. When the profit goal is reached, the position is closed.

Another popular general approach is trailing stops. The idea with a trailing stop is that the exit price point moves up with the upward price movement of the stock. This keeps the trader in the rising stock until the price begins to fall back and reaches the trailing stop, where the position is closed.

These two profit-taking exits can be used in combination. Once the profit target price is reached, some proportion of the total position (e.g., half) can be closed and a trailing stop set for the remaining part of the position.

LOSS-BASED EXITS

The most important exit is a money management stop-loss, designed to address the worst case scenario. This stop is your "line in the sand." If the stock price falls to this level, you will automatically close your position. You should decide upon this stop-loss before entering the trade. In fact, I recommend that once each of your stock entry orders is filled you immediately enter your money management exit stop using a "Good 'Til Cancelled" (GTC) order.

> "No one bats 1,000. Even Warren Buffet is right only 70 per cent of the time. Mistakes are just part of the process. You just have to admit your mistakes – and perhaps set stop-loss orders."
> -- John Longo

Some people are reluctant to enter a stop-loss order with their broker, fearing that the market makers will use the information to drive the stock price down to hit the stop price and close their position with a loss, then allow the price to rise again while they are on the sidelines with no position in the stock.

While this fear may be justified in some cases, it is unfounded for most traders. If the market maker was manipulating the price as described above, it would be the very large positions of extremely wealthy traders or institutions that would be the target, not the stop-loss points of the typical trader.

A mental stop is a price point that you decide will be your "line in the sand," but you do not enter it into your brokerage account. I strongly recommend against using a "mental stop-loss." Although it would prevent the possibility of the market manipulation described above targeting you, it still is not a good plan.

While you can have an alert sent to your email and/or phone, multiple circumstances can lead to a significant time lag between the alert being sent and you being able to actually execute your exit order. Consequently, your actual exit price could be significantly lower than the mental stop-loss that you had planned to use.

Finally, you could monitor the prices of all the stocks that you own during the entire trading day (a time investment of 6.5 hours per trading day), but that plan would be unacceptable to many people.

Even if you are willing to make the time investment, human psychology can work against actually exiting at your planned stop-loss point. If the stock price falls to the mental stop-loss price level, people will frequently rationalize that they have done sound research in picking the stock and that the price will turn around and go up.

Even worse, when the price falls through your mental stop price and continues down, you will have the same decision to make the next day, but with a smaller balance in your trading account. This rationalization process can sometimes go on for days, with a decreasing account balance each day.

At some point, most traders will finally give up, sell their losing position at a much greater loss than their original mental stop price level, and be left with a negative view on the value of stock trading, perhaps even completely abandoning their hopes of being a successful stock trader.

Given the importance of using a stop-loss for all your open positions, how should a stop-loss price be determined? Dr. Bart DiLiddo addressed this important question in the February 20, 2009 edition of the *VectorVest Views*.

He offered a formula for determining a stop-loss percent which takes into account a combination of various money management issues including: the percent risk of loss for a single stock position, the number of positions held in the portfolio, and the percent of the trading account funds that are invested. His formula is shown in equation {3} below:

$$\{3\} \ S = (100 * R * N) / C$$

where:

    S is the stop-loss percent;

    R is the percent risk of loss for a single stock position;

    N is the number of positions in the portfolio; and,

    C is the percent of capital that is invested.

To illustrate the application of this equation, suppose that our goal is to keep our percent loss on any single stock position at 1%. Further, we plan to have five different stocks in our portfolio and use only 50% of our total account funds for the five positions. Substituting into the above formula:

$$S = (100 * 1 * 5) / 50$$
$$= (500) / 50$$
$$= 10$$

We would set our stop-loss percent at 10% to achieve our goal.

If examination of the stock's volatility suggests that a 10% stop-loss will be triggered frequently, we might want to use a 20% stop-loss point to give the position more breathing room. This could be accomplished by investing only 50% of our funds and still meet our goal of keeping our percent loss on a single stock to 1% by raising the five positions in the previous example to ten positions. Substituting these figures into the equation gives:

$$S = (100 * 1 * 10) / 50$$
$$= (1000) / 50$$
$$= 20$$

By providing greater diversification with the ten positions, we can afford to give each individual stock more freedom to move, and still maintain our goal of keeping our percent loss on a single position set at 1%, while still using only half our total capital for investment.

Suppose we were very aggressive and wanted to have all our account funds invested but we still wanted to keep our percent loss on a single stock at 1%. We could accomplish this by having a stop-loss of 10% as long as we use ten positions:

$$S = (100 * 1 * 10) / 100$$
$$= (1000) / 100$$
$$= 10$$

TIME-BASED EXITS

When you have entered a trade, you expect to make a profit in a reasonable timeframe. If the price of your stock essentially stays the same over an extended period of time, the position should be closed. Each and every day that your funds are tied up with the stagnant stock, you incur an opportunity cost. You could be using those funds to invest in a stock that is moving in price and generating a profit. Patience is not always a virtue in stock trading.

CONCLUSION

Planning and following a sound exit strategy is essential to your trading success over the long run. I offer you the following suggestions:

Formulate your exit plan before you enter stock positions, not in the

> "We are what we repeatedly do. Excellence, then, is not an act but a habit."
>
> -- Aristotle

"heat of battle" when the market is open and prices are moving very fast.

Include your money and risk management considerations in planning the exit price points.

Do not use mental stop-losses. Use "hard" stop-loss exits that are entered with your broker and will be executed automatically, without your vigilance and intervention.

Consider having both a profit exit and a loss exit for each open position. The best setting for your exit(s) should be determined by thorough backtesting on historical data.

And, finally:

Follow Your Plan!

Trading Records

"I think it's important to note that we really did try hard."

TRADING RECORDS

OVERVIEW

Conscientious recording of your stock market trade information is important for many reasons. From a legal standpoint, you will need documentation for tax filing purposes. In addition, detailed information on your trades is essential for your self-assessment, evaluation, and improvement of your trading skills. This, in turn, will provide you with the ability to learn what you are doing right and, perhaps more important, what you are doing wrong.

> "Record-keeping is important. Document everything you do."
> -- Frank Degan

TRADING DIARY

The purpose of your trading diary is to record information on your perceptions and the actions that you take in your trading account(s). This diary will include your subjective opinions and perspective surrounding your trading actions. Data elements in your trading diary should include at least the following information:

- Stock Symbol

- Date

- Action

- Overall Market Conditions

- Business Sector Conditions

- Industry Group Conditions

- Stock Conditions

- Profit Target Price

- Stop-Loss Price

STOCK CHARTS

Many traders find it helpful to include a chart of each stock traded showing the conditions at position entry and a second chart showing the conditions at position exit. You can also include charts showing different timeframes (e.g., intra-day, daily, weekly) to give you alternative perspectives.

These charts can be annotated with your personal notes (e.g., marking support and resistance). Taken together, the charts and accompanying narratives will provide key information for you to review and use to improve your trading in the future.

STOCK TRADE INFORMATION

You should record information for each individual trade that you make. This performance record will cover <u>objective data</u> on your trading actions. Four types of data are involved: trade entry, trade exit, individual trade performance, and cumulative trade performance.

Trade Entry Data

You should record the following information every time you open a stock position:

- Trade Sequence Number (e.g., 001, 002, ..., nnn)

- Trade ID Number (e.g., YYYY-001, YYYY-002, etc.)

- Trading Account

- Stock Symbol

- Number Shares

- Entry Date

- Entry Price Per Share

- Entry Commission

- Total Entry Amount

Trade Exit Data

After you close a stock position, you should record the following information:

- Exit Date

- Exit Price Per Share

- Exit Commission

- Total Exit Amount

Individual Trade Performance Data

Each individual trade can be evaluated based upon the following criteria:

- Followed Your Rules (Yes/No)?

- Profit / Loss Amount

- Profit / Loss Percent

- Days in Trade

- Annualized Return Rate

- Maximum Drawdown

Cumulative Trade Performance Data

In addition to recording information for each individual trade, you need an ongoing, cumulative record for assessing your performance. Cumulative trade performance data could include:

- Number of Trades

- Days in Trades

- Total Profit (or Loss) Amount

- Total Profit (or Loss) Percent

- Annualized Return Rate

- Maximum Drawdown

DISCUSSION

Most of the stock trade information listed above is familiar to everyone. However, three of the data elements merit discussion:

- Followed Your Rules (Yes/No)?

- Annualized Return Rate

- Maximum Drawdown

Did You Follow Your Trading Rules?

The first data element in evaluating the performance of an individual trade is whether or not you followed your rules in conducting the trade. With two actions (Rules: followed vs. not followed) and two outcomes (Final Value of Trade: profit vs. loss), there are four possible decision-outcome combinations, as shown in Table 5:

Table 5: Possible Decision-Outcome Combinations

		Rules	
		Followed	*Not Followed*
Final Dollar Value of Trade	*Profit*	A	C
	Loss	B	D

Obviously, the best combination is A, where the trader followed his rules (reinforcing a disciplined approach) and achieved a profit. Clearly, the worst combination is D, where the trader did not follow his rules (not following a disciplined approach) and suffered a losing trade.

The second best combination is not as obvious. Some would argue that the C combination

> "The only mistake in life is the lesson not learned."
> -- Albert Einstein

is the second best because any trade that is profitable is better than a losing trade. I disagree with that perspective. I think that the second best combination is B because the trader is reinforcing a disciplined approach to trading which will serve him well in the long run. This discipline is more important than the loss on a single trade.

Annualized Return Rate

The Annualized Return Rate (ARR) extrapolates a Return Rate achieved in a period other than an exact year to a precise annual rate. Phrased another way, ARR answers the question, "What would be the percent return (or loss) if you had achieved the same return rate for exactly one year?" Annualized Return Rate allows you to place multiple trades with varying time in the trades onto the same metric, facilitating comparisons.

There are a number of different formulas for calculating the Annualized Rate of Return. It is important to understand that the purpose of the extrapolation is to place return rates achieved in different numbers of days onto a common metric, so that they can be rank-ordered from best to worst.

Note that you must use the same formula in all of your calculations of ARR. As long as the alternative trade results are all extrapolated using the same method, the rank-ordering of trades will be the same. That is, you will be comparing apples to apples and oranges to oranges.

I use the following simple method, which has two big advantages over some other methods of calculating ARR. First, it makes intuitive sense. In addition, this method does not involve any exponentiation and is easily performed with any basic calculator:

$$\{4\}\ ARR = 100 * [(EA\ /\ BA) - 1] * [DY\ /\ DT]$$

where:

ARR is the Annualized Return Rate;

EA is the Ending Amount;

BA is the Beginning Amount;

DY is the number of Days in the Year (use 360 or 365); and,

DT is the number of Days in the Trade.

As mentioned above, this simple formula produces an intuitively correct answer. For example, suppose that a trade began with $10,000 on March 1, 2011 and ended with $11,500 on August 28, 2011. The Return Rate would be 15% achieved in 180 days (half a year). Obviously, extrapolating this to a full year (using 360 days in a year) would be an Annualized Return Rate (ARR) of 30%. To illustrate the use of equation {4}, we substitute these values and solve for the Annualized Return Rate:

$$= 100 * [(\$11{,}500 / \$10{,}000) - 1] * [360 / 180]$$
$$= 100 * [1.15 - 1.00] * [2]$$
$$= 100 * [0.15] * [2]$$
$$= 100 * 0.30$$
$$= 30\%$$

In this example, the entry and exit dates produced a trade that was held for exactly 50% of a year. Obviously, to extrapolate the results out to a full year, we would just double the half-year results.

However, most actual trades will be difficult to assess correctly without using the ARR equation. Once we have the ARR for each trade, we can compare them on an "apples to apples" basis. To illustrate, suppose that we have the three trades shown in Table 6.

Table 6: Trade Periods and Amounts for Three Example Trades

Trade	Beginning Date	Beginning Amount	Ending Date	Ending Amount
A	02/06/2012	$10,264	09/19/2012	$11,627
B	04/26/2012	$7,600	12/28/2012	$8,819
C	05/15/2012	$15,725	8/03/2012	$16,700

Using the information in Table 6, we can determine the Profit/Loss Amount for the three example trades, as shown in Table 7:

Table 7: Profit/Loss Amount and Rank for Three Example Trades

Trade	Profit/Loss Amount	Trade Rank
A	+$1,363	1
B	+$1,219	2
C	+$975	3

Clearly, using the Profit/Loss Amount as the measure of trade performance, Trade A was the best trade, and Trade C was the worst trade.

However, noting that the amount invested in each trade in Table 6 is different, we could use the Profit/Loss Percent to rank-order the three trades, as shown in Table 8:

Table 8: Profit/Loss Percent and Rank for Three Example Trades

Trade	Profit/Loss Percent	Trade Rank
A	+13.28%	2
B	+16.04%	1
C	+6.20%	3

Now, based upon the profit/loss percent realized by the three trades, we might conclude that Trade B was the best trade, with Trade C being the worst trade.

However, this is still not the best way of evaluating the alternative trades because we were in the trades for varying lengths of time. Table 9 shows the three trades rank-ordered by the Annualized Return Rate.

Table 9: Annualized Return Rate And Rank For Three Example Trades

Trade	Annualized Return Rate	Trade Rank
A	21.15%	3
B	23.47%	2
C	27.90%	1

Rank-ordering the three trades based on the Annualized Return Rate, we see that the best trade was actually Trade C, while the worst trade was Trade A. This conclusion would have been difficult to see unless we calculated the Annualized Return Rate for the three trades. Every trade involves potential reward and potential risk. The Annualized Return Rate represents the reward side of the reward-risk balance.

Maximum Drawdown

The maximum drawdown is the largest decrease in equity from a peak in the equity curve to the next equity valley. This is important because the maximum drawdown may be greater than a trader can tolerate, causing him to "bail out" and exit a position. This can occur in a trade that, if it hadn't been closed, would have resulted in a large profit. Just evaluating the final outcome does not acknowledge the level of discomfort that accompanies a large equity drawdown. The Maximum Drawdown represents the risk side of the reward-risk balance.

CUMULATIVE EQUITY CURVE

If you are tracking your portfolio performance in an automated system, you can probably display and print out a portfolio equity curve showing your performance over time. This equity graph will provide a perspective that augments your understanding and interpretation of the various numbers mentioned above. You should track your cumulative trade performance against your trading goals specified in your Mission Statement, described in a previous section. Based on this comparison, you may decide to modify your trading rules, your goals, or both.

EVALUATION SCHEDULE

The schedule that you adopt for reviewing your trading performance will be based upon the amount of time you choose to devote to understanding and improving that performance. This could include a daily, weekly, monthly, quarterly, and annual review. Reviewing your performance should never take place when the stock market is open and you are trading, as it will interfere with your concentration and direct your focus away from current trading activities.

VALUE OF TRADING RECORDS

We have covered a lot of ground in this Trading Records section. While the recordkeeping may seem to be an onerous burden, it will provide you with the information to assess your progress, identify the lessons to be learned, and improve your trading performance.

Launching Your Trading Success

Tech stocks were up and so was Jeffrey.

Image Copyright Cartoonresource, 2013
Used under license from Shutterstock.com

LAUNCHING YOUR TRADING SUCCESS

Treat your stock trading as a business, a serious financial endeavor that can reap tremendous benefits or devastating losses. Your trading plan is your key to trading success. Developing, maintaining, and periodically reviewing your trading plan is important for consistent, long-term profitable performance.

Comparing your actual performance against your trading plan goals provides you with the information feedback needed to make changes, both to your trading rules and to your trading plan objectives. Your trading plan is a living document that you can (and should) change and improve over time.

Never forget that you are the key to your trading success. Your trading plan is a tool for you to use in achieving that success. You must maintain the self-discipline to follow your plan. Recall the famous quote from the Pogo comic strip: "We have met the enemy and he is us." Trading by your set of rules according to your trading plan will go a long way towards preventing the losses caused by trading on your emotions.

The development and maintenance of your trading plan will involve a time investment on your part. Keep in mind that the time you spend is an investment in yourself and the future financial well-being of you and your loved ones.

> "Plan Your Trade. Trade Your Plan."
> -- Author Unknown

In conclusion, I wish you every success in your stock trading and believe that the information provided in this book will help you to achieve your stock market trading goals.

Trade By Rules,

Drew Sands

Contact: StockMarketProfits@TradeByRules.com

REFERENCES

DiLiddo, B. *VectorVest Views: Overview*, February 6, 2009.

DiLiddo, B. *VectorVest Views: Overview*, February 20, 2009.

Hirsch, Y. & Brown, J.T. *The Almanac Investor: Profit from Market History and Seasonal Trends*. Hoboken, NJ: John Wiley & Sons, Inc., 2006.

LeBeau, C. & Lucas, D. W. *Technical Traders Guide to Computer Analysis of the Futures Market*. New York: McGraw-Hill, 1992.

Tharp, V. K. *Trade Your Way to Financial Freedom*. New York: McGrawHill, 1999.

GLOSSARY

Account Executive – the individual who has the responsibility for managing a brokerage account.

Active Trades – trades in which there are open positions.

Advance-Decline Line – an indicator that measures the breadth of the market by tracking the number of advancing and declining stocks.

Affordable Risk – the amount of investment money that a trader can afford to lose without seriously compromising the trader's lifestyle.

Aggressive – an investment strategy that has a high profit goal and accepts an above-average level of risk. The goal of an aggressive strategy is capital appreciation.

Aggressive – Conservative Continuum – a range of trading or investing styles. See **Aggressive** and **Conservative**.

All-In – an entry strategy wherein the entire number of shares that an individual plans to purchase is purchased as one single trade. See **Scaling-In** for another entry approach.

All-Out – an exit strategy wherein all the shares in an open stock position are exited as a single trade. See **Scaling-Out** for another exit approach

Analysis Paralysis – a situation where a trader has multiple indicators that are providing conflicting guidance which results in an inability to make a decision and take action.

Annualized Return Rate (ARR) – the rate of return for a given period of time is extrapolated to the return rate that would have been achieved if the investment had been held for exactly one year. The ARR makes possible a fair comparison of multiple investments held for different periods of time.

At The Market Sell Order – an order to sell stock at the current market price if the market is open. If the market is closed, this order will be executed at the existing price when the market opens. This type of order guarantees execution (i.e., the stock will be sold), but does not guarantee a certain price.

Average True Range – the average of the true ranges over a specified number of trading periods (e.g., days). The range is defined as the difference between the high and low prices of a stock during the trading period. As such, the range does not take gaps from the previous period into account. The true range includes a consideration of price gaps, and is defined as the maximum of the following three price differences: (1) high minus low of the current period (the range), (2) high of the current period minus the close of the previous period, and (3) the close of the previous period minus the low of the current period.

Averaging Down – a procedure that buys some shares at a particular price and then buys additional shares after the price falls, thereby lowering the average cost of the entire position. This is a risky strategy. If the price continues to fall, the trader has more dollars in the losing position than would be the case if the second purchase had not occurred. See **Averaging Up**.

Averaging Up – a procedure that buys some shares at a particular price and then buys additional shares after the price rises, thereby raising the average cost of the entire position. This is a safer strategy than averaging down. The downside of this strategy is that if the entire position in the stock had been purchased at the original price, the average price would be lower and the profit would be greater if the stock price rises. See **Averaging Down**.

Back Testing – testing a trading strategy on historical data to evaluate the performance characteristics of the strategy (profit/loss, maximum drawdown, etc.).

Bear Market – a substantial decline in the stock market as a whole. While there is no one operational definition of a bear market that is universally accepted, one popular definition is a decrease of 20 percent or more. See **Bull Market**.

Bearish Position – a position that was chosen with the expectation of lower prices. See **Bullish Position**.

Break – a point where the price of a stock suddenly plunges downward. This sudden dramatic price loss can cause traders to sell in a panic, thereby accelerating the price decline.

Breakout – occurs when the price of a stock shifts outside of a range that has previously contained price movements.

Break-even Point – the price where there is neither a profit nor a loss for the position.

Brokerage Account – cash that has been transferred and entrusted to a securities brokerage.

Bull Market – a substantial rise in the stock market as a whole. The stock market often leads the general economy in direction and this price rise often begins before signs of economic recovery are observed. See **Bear Market**.

Bullish Position – a position that was chosen with the expectation of higher prices. See **Bearish Position**.

Business Sector – a broad segment of the overall market that includes multiple smaller and more focused industry groups of stocks. For example, "Food" is a business sector that contains the industry group "Candy." See **Industry Group**.

Buy and Hold Strategy – an investment strategy that buys stock and holds onto that stock for a long period of time, ignoring the short-term price fluctuations. This strategy assumes that the market as a whole will rise over a long period of time and that the stocks in the portfolio will benefit from that overall upward trend of the market.

Buy Stop Price – a price that is entered with a broker to buy a specified number of shares of a stock if, and when, the stock price reaches that level.

Calendar Patterns – stock market or individual stock price patterns that are based upon calendar dates.

Composite Score – score based upon a combination of two or more component scores.

Conservative – an investment strategy that has moderate profit goals and accepts only a limited level of risk. A conservative strategy emphasizes capital preservation.

Contra-Trend – a strategy that trades against the existing trend. For example, if the trend of a stock is up, a contra-trend trade would be betting that the up-trend will not continue and that the price will reverse and start to move down.

Convergence – occurs when two separate measures approach the same level. An example is the price of a stock and the value of that stock can be significantly different for a period of time and then approach the same price level. See **Divergence**.

Correction – occurs when the price of a stock rises (or falls) very rapidly and then begins to move back toward the original price. An example is a stock that releases an earnings report showing results that far exceed expectations which prompts a tremendous number of investors and traders to buy shares in the stock, thereby causing the price to rise substantially. However, once this initial flurry of buying ceases, the stock price begins to fall back towards the initial price.

Day Trading – a trading strategy that opens and closes stock positions in the same day. Typically, the day trader will see an opportunity, enter a large position, watch the price improve a relatively small amount, and then exit the position before any price correction takes place. The trader may enter and exit positions in the same stock many times during the same day. The defining characteristic of a day trader is always closing out all positions before the end of the trading day. This protects the trader from any events that occur while the market is closed that would adversely impact the stock price.

Days in Trade – the number of days a trade is open. When evaluating the results of a trade, it is necessary to take into account the number of days in the trade, in addition to the profit or loss of a trade. See **Annual Return Rate**.

Discretionary Account – a brokerage account that allows a designated individual to make and implement trading decisions without the consent of the account owner for the individual decisions. This type of account is established with an upfront agreement where the account owner agrees to give the designated person that authority.

Discretionary Trading – a trading style in which decisions are based upon the trader's opinion. This style can be contrasted with rule-based trading, wherein the trading decisions are based upon an explicit rule (or set of rules).

Divergence – a situation where two measures move apart in price. An example is a stock price that rises to a level considerably above the current value of that stock. Another example would be when the stock price increases and a technical analysis indicator decreases.

Diversified Portfolio – a portfolio containing a variety of investments that move relatively independently in price (i.e., the individual investments have a low correlation). The goal of a diversified portfolio is to mitigate the unsystematic risk of each individual security so that the portfolio risk is about the same as the overall market systematic risk.

Dow-Jones Industrial Average – price-weighted average of 30 of the best blue-chip companies that trade on the New York Stock Exchange and the NASDAQ. This index is widely followed as a measure of "the market," despite the fact that these 30 stocks are not representative of all the stocks in the stock market.

Down-Market Periods – periods of time when the price of the overall market is heading down.

Earnings Per Share (EPS) – a measure of the profits of a company. The EPS is calculated as the profit minus the dividends paid divided by the number of outstanding shares.

Entry – opening a position in a stock.

Entry Rules – the rules a trader follows to decide the conditions required to enter a stock position.

Entry Strategy – the strategy a trader employs to open stock positions.

Equal-Dollar Amount – a strategy that invests an equal amount of money in each different stock in a portfolio, resulting in a different number of shares of each stock. This approach is often contrasted with a strategy that buys an equal number of shares of each stock in the portfolio, resulting in a different amount of money invested in each stock.

Equity – the total assets of a portfolio minus the total liabilities. This is the total amount of money the individual would keep after closing all positions and paying off any margin loan liabilities and transaction fees.

Equity Curve – a chart that shows the cumulative profit/loss of the portfolio over a specified time period.

Equity Peak – a high point of a chart that shows the equity curve.

Equity Valley – a low point of a chart that shows the equity curve.

Execution – the fulfillment of a trade order.

Exit – the closing of an open stock position. If the position is a long position, the exit involves selling the shares. If the position is a short position, the exit involves buying the shares (covering) that were originally borrowed from the broker and sold to open the short position and returning them to the broker.

Exit Rule – the exact condition or conditions that, when met, signal that an open position should be closed.

Exponential Moving Average – a type of moving average that places more weight on the most recent price than on the prices of earlier time periods. This approach reflects a belief that recent prices are more important than historical prices. An exponential moving average will track price movement more closely than a **Simple Moving Average**, based on the same number of trading periods (e.g., days).

Exponentiation – a mathematical operation involving two numbers: a base number (n) and an exponent (b). The exponent is normally shown as a superscript and is displayed to the right of the base number (n^b). It is normally read as "n raised to the bth power).

Extrapolate – using existing data points to construct new data points outside the range of the existing data points.

Fade – a bet in the opposite direction of the current price movement. An example is buying a stock that is rapidly falling in price.

Fill – the completed execution of a trade order.

Fundamental Analysis – an approach to trading that is based upon a company's financial performance (e.g., earnings). See **Technical Analysis** for an alternative approach.

Fundamentals – factors that are used to evaluate the success potential of a company. Examples of fundamental factors include earnings, cash flow, etc.

Good 'Til Canceled (GTC) Order – an order to buy or sell a stock that remains operational until it is either executed or cancelled. Frequently, a brokerage company allows the order to stay active for a long period of time, but not forever. At the end of that period of time, the trader can renew the order.

Hypothetical Trade – a trade that is not actually placed, but is treated as if it were an actual trade. Paper trading involves hypothetical trades. Data are collected on these hypothetical trades and evaluated to assess the efficacy of a trading strategy or trading system. This allows the assessment to be completed without risking any real money.

Index – a number that characterizes an entire group of stocks. In some indices, the component stocks are all treated equally, while other indices weight the component stocks differently (e.g., based on capitalization). See **Weighted Stock Index**.

Industry Group – a focused segment of the overall market that includes stocks with very similar products (e.g., Candy). Related industry groups can be aggregated into a broader group called a **Business Sector** (e.g., Food).

Inflation – a significant rise in the cost of living that is related to the loss in the value of currency caused by increasing the amount of currency in circulation.

Interest Rate – the lender of an asset charges the borrower for the use of those assets. The interest rate is the amount of money charged as a percent of the amount borrowed.

Leverage – using borrowed money to control a larger quantity of assets (e.g., shares of stocks) than you could control with your own money alone. The use of leverage magnifies the potential profit and the potential loss. This magnification has led to leverage being characterized as a "double-edged sword."

Limit Order – an order placed with the brokerage company to buy at the limit price or better for a long position, or sell at the limit price or better for a short position. A limit order guarantees a price but does not guarantee the execution of the order. See **Market Order.**

Line in the Sand – a figure of speech indicating a price that someone is not willing to change. For example, an individual wants to sell his shares of stock and is not willing to take any price below his "line in the sand" price.

Living Document – a dynamic document that is designed to be updated as additional evidence becomes available, rather than being a static, "set in stone" document that never changes.

Long Trading Strategy – a strategy wherein the trader buys stock anticipating a price rise that produces a profit. The opposite type of strategy is a **Short Trading Strategy.**

Loss Exit – closing a trade at a price that results in a loss.

Margin – the equity amount invested by an individual (e.g., cash) as a percentage of the total market value of the stock purchased. For example, when the margin rate is 50%, a broker may allow a trader to buy $100,000 of stock for $50,000 and lend the trader $50,000.

Margin Account – a type of trading account with a brokerage company. In this type of account, the broker has approved the trader for something similar to an open line of credit, and the broker lends the pre-approved trader money to assist in the purchase of stocks. For example, if a trader wants to purchase $100,000 of a stock, and the margin rate is 50%, the trader can make the purchase if he has $50,000 in his account. The broker lends the trader the other $50,000 needed to complete the purchase. The trader is charged a margin rate fee for the loan.

Market Forecasting – the prediction of future stock market price behavior.

Market Order – an order to be executed as soon as possible at the current stock price.

Market Timing – using technical analysis and/or calendar-based patterns to identify up and down market trends. This information can be used to make decisions on when to enter and when to exit stock positions.

Market Timing System – a system of rules for identifying up and down trends in the market. This information is used to make decisions on when to enter and when to exit stock positions.

Maximum Drawdown – the greatest percent loss between a peak price and a subsequent low price during a specified time period.

Mental Stop-Loss – stop-loss price point that is established by the trader but not entered as an order with the brokerage account. The trader plans on monitoring prices and entering an exit order when the mental stop price is reached.

Mission Statement – a written document that specifies the goals for a business, the approach that will be employed to achieve the goals, and the means of evaluating progress toward achievement of the goals.

Momentum – the difference between the closing price today and the closing price N days ago. Momentum is a trend-following technical analysis indicator which remains positive during an uptrend and remains negative during a downtrend.

Money Management – the procedures used to make decisions on asset allocation and risk control.

NASDAQ – an acronym that represents a major U.S. stock exchange which emphasizes large, high quality technical stocks. Originally the acronym stood for the National Association of Security Dealers Automated Quotation.

NASDAQ 100 Index – an index representing the 100 largest companies listed on the **NASDAQ** (excluding bank stocks).

Open Short – an open position that will be profitable if the price falls below the entry price. For example, a trader opens a short position by borrowing shares of a stock from the broker and selling them for $45. If the price falls to $35, the trader buys the shares in the market, returns them to the broker, and realizes the profit ($10); i.e., the difference between the opening selling price and the closing buy price (ignoring transaction costs).

Overbought – a situation where the price of a stock has risen to an extreme point where everyone who wanted to buy the stock has done so. With no one left to buy shares, the price will begin to decline. See **Oversold**.

Over-fitting – occurs when the rules of a trading strategy are designed to fit the characteristics of a sample of data so closely that they cannot be used to successfully make predictions about another sample. Ideally, a study will identify the characteristics of a sample that will represent other samples (the "signal"), but not capture the idiosyncratic characteristics of the sample which will not be useful in making predictions about another sample (the "noise"), thereby avoiding over-fitting.

Oversold – a situation where the price of a stock has fallen to an extreme point where everyone who wanted to sell has done so. With no one left to sell shares, the price will begin to rise. See **Overbought**.

Paper Trade – a hypothetical or virtual trade that does not involve actual money but is managed as if it were a real trade.

Performance Evaluation Metrics – measures used to evaluate performance (e.g., **Annualized Return Rate**).

Portfolio – a collection of stocks that are traded within a single account.

Portfolio Risk – the amount of risk a trader is willing to accept for the planned trading strategy.

Position Sizing – the amount of money invested in a position.

Profit/Loss Amount – the amount of money gained or lost in a trade.

Profit/Loss Percent – the percentage of gain or loss realized in a trade, calculated as: 100 * [(Ending Dollar Amount – Starting Dollar Amount) / Starting Dollar Amount].

Profit Exit – a profit target which, when reached, triggers a position exit.

Profit Objective – a goal for profit that, when reached, gives a signal to exit the trade.

Qualified Candidates – stocks that meet all the minimum standards established for being considered for inclusion into the portfolio.

Random – something that occurs by chance; i.e., it cannot be accurately predicted in a consistent way.

Random Walk – a theory maintains that there is no consistent relationship between a stock's prices at two different points in time and, therefore, that prices cannot be predicted as they move in reaction to the inflow of buy and sell orders. A statistical description is that there is no significant correlation between sequential stock prices (i.e., that the prices are independent of one another).

Relative Safety (RS) – A VectorVest proprietary indicator that describes a stock's risk, based upon the consistency of the stock's financial performance.

Relative Strength – a measure of a stock's performance compared to a market index or another stock. For example, the relative strength of a stock can be calculated by dividing the 52-week rate of change for the stock by the 52-week rate of change of the S&P-500 index. Typically, this result is multiplied by 100.

Relative Timing (RT) – A VectorVest proprietary indicator that describes a stock's price trend.

Relative Value (RV) – A VectorVest proprietary indicator that describes the long-term potential of a stock for price appreciation.

Resistance – a price or price zone where, on multiple occasions, a rising stock price stops its upward movement and begins to fall. The resistance level is shown by a horizontal line drawn on a chart. See **Support**.

Return Rate – the profit or loss on an investment during a specified period of time, divided by the original investment amount. The rate of return is usually expressed as a percentage. See **Annual Return Rate**.

Risk – the probability that an investment will result in a loss. Investment opportunities with the goal of high returns generally also have a high risk of loss.

Risk Capital – the amount of money that a trader can afford to risk without having a serious adverse impact on the trader's standard of living. See **Affordable Risk**.

Risk Tolerance – the financial and psychological ability of a trader to accept both actual and potential losses from an investment. Generally speaking, an aggressive stock strategy that has high percent gains as the goal will require a high risk tolerance, while a conservative strategy with a lower profit goal will require a lower risk tolerance.

Rule-Based Trading – the type of trading that uses one or more objectively defined rules to make trading strategy decisions.

S&P-500 – see Standard & Poor's 500 Index.

Scaling-In – an entry approach where the total number of shares that are planned for purchase is broken into two or more pieces for separate trades. See **All-In** for the alternative method.

Scaling-Out – an exit approach wherein the total number of shares in a position are exited in two or more phases. See **All-Out** for an alternative approach.

Screening – a process where each individual stock in a universe of stocks is evaluated based upon one or more criteria. Those stocks that meet all the screening criteria are considered to be "**Qualified Candidates**" for investment.

Short Trading Strategy – a trading strategy wherein the trader borrows stock from the broker, sells the stock with the goal of buying it back later at a lower price and returning the borrowed stock to the broker. The difference between the original selling price and the price required to buy back the stock is the profit (or loss) to the trader (ignoring transaction and margin costs).

Simple Moving Average – an arithmetic average of prices in a fixed-length period. For example, the average closing price for the last five days would be calculated by adding together the closing prices for the last five days and dividing that total by five. The moving average is tracked by moving the fixed-length period each day. This means that the latest closing price is added into the total and the oldest closing price is subtracted from that total. This new, updated value is based on the most recent five-day period. This type of moving average is called simple because the closing prices are not weighted differently, implying that they all are equally important. See **Exponential Moving Average**.

Standard & Poor's 500 Index – a market value weighted index of a collection of 500 widely held U.S stocks. The S&P-500 is widely regarded as one of the best indicators of the U.S. stock market. The symbol SPY can be used to trade this broad basket of stocks with a single transaction fee.

Stock Entry – when a stock position is opened.

Stock Exit – when a stock position is closed.

Stock Market Indices – indices that are designed to represent the stock market as a whole with a single number. These indices frequently serve as benchmarks for evaluating the performance of stock trading systems.

Stock Risk – the amount of money that a trader decides can be risked on a single stock. This amount is the difference between the entry price and the stop-loss price multiplied by the number of shares, not the total amount invested in the stock.

Stock Screening – a process of evaluating each stock in a list to determine the best candidates for investment. For example, evaluating each stock in the Standard & Poors 500 stocks according to a set of qualification rules and identifying those stocks that meet all the rules. See **Screening** and **Qualified Candidates**.

Stock Selection – the process of choosing those stocks that a trader wants to buy for a portfolio from among a list of "**Qualified Candidates**."

Stop Loss Exit Price – a price entered with a broker to exit a trader's position if the stock price reaches that stop-loss level. The purpose is to limit the loss of funds as the stock price moves against the trader.

Stop Loss Order – an order to the broker to exit a trader's stock position if the price reaches a specified level. This type of order is used to exit a losing position before the loss becomes greater.

Stop Order – an order to buy or sell a stock once a specified price level is reached or exceeded. Once this occurs, the order becomes a market order that will be executed at the current market price.

Stop-Limit Order – a combination of a stop order and a limit order. Once the stop price has been reached or surpassed, this order will be executed at the specified limit price (or better).

Support – a price or price zone where a falling stock price stops the downward movement on multiple occasions and begins to rise. The support level is shown by a horizontal line drawn on a chart. See the term **Resistance**.

Technical Analysis – an approach to trading that relies on the price and volume behavior of a stock (or the market as a whole). Frequently, charts are used to portray the price behavior in an effort to predict price trends. See **Fundamental Analysis** for an alternative approach.

Time-Based Exit – an order to exit an open stock position if a sufficient profit has not been achieved during a specified time period. This type of exit is designed to avoid tying up funds in a stock that is not moving in the desired direction so that the money may be invested in a more promising stock.

Top Down Approach – a stock trading approach that starts with the overall stock market, then analyzes the broad business sectors, then the more focused industry groups and, finally, the individual stocks.

Trading Diary – a record of the trader's perceptions and subjective opinions on the entry and exit conditions for every trade.

Trading Plan – a business plan for trading activities.

Trading Platform Software – the program on the trader's computer that allows trading activities to take place over the internet.

Trailing Stop – an order to exit a long position at a specified percent or dollar drop from the highest of the entry price or the highest price reached since the position was opened. A trailing stop for a short position would exit the trade at a specified percent or dollar rise from the lowest of the entry price or the lowest price reached since the short position was opened.

Trend – the overall direction of the stock market or an individual stock.

Trend-Following – a trading strategy that identifies stocks that are trending as candidates for investment.

Turbulence – fast and significant up and down stock price movements.

VectorVest – founded by Dr. Bart DiLiddo, this company provides extensive stock trading information on their website (VectorVest.com), their software platforms, and through their education and training seminars offered around the world.

VectorVest Composite (VST) – a VectorVest proprietary composite indicator based upon the **Relative Value (RV)**, **Relative Safety (RS)**, and **Relative Timing (RT)** indicators. The VST is used to rank-order all the stocks in the VectorVest database in terms of overall investment potential.

Virtual Money – fictitious money that only exists in cyberspace. Virtual money is used in a **Paper Trade** to simulate the procedures and consequences of trading a stock system, without risking any real money.

Volatility – a statistical measure of variation in the price of a stock. Stocks with a high degree of volatility are considered more risky than those with a smaller volatility.

Volume – the number of stock shares traded during a specified period of time (e.g., a day).

VST – see VectorVest Composite.

Weighted Stock Index – a stock index where the components are weighted differently. When a stock index is not weighted, the price of each component stock is added to get a total and that total is divided by the number of stocks to yield an average stock price. In contrast, a weighted stock index involves assigning each of the component stocks a different weight based upon some characteristic of that stock (e.g., capitalization).

Whipsaw – a situation where the trader opens a position in a stock in a particular direction (e.g., up), only to see the price go in the opposite direction (down). This adverse price movement causes the trader to close the position at a loss. Then the trader, following the most recent price move direction (down), opens a new short position. The price then reverses again (rises) and, again, the trader exits the latest position at a loss.

Yield – the interest or dividend paid to the trader by the stock company. Typically, the yield amount is divided by the investment cost and expressed as a percentage.

Annotated Recommended Books

Appel, Gerald. *Technical Analysis: Power Tools for Active Investors.* Upper Saddle River, NJ: Financial Times Prentice Hall, 2005.

For traders employing technical analysis, written by the creator of the widely used Moving Average Convergence-Divergence (MACD) indicator.

Arms, Richard W. Jr. *The Arms Index (TRIN): An Introduction to the Volume Analysis of Stock and Bond Markets.* Columbia MD: Marketplace Books, 1989.

A classic book by the originator of the Arms Index (TRIN) technical analysis indicator.

Balsara, Nauzer J. *Money Management Strategies for Futures Traders.* New York: John Wiley & Sons, 1992.

An excellent book on money management and risk control in trading.

Barnes, Robert M. *Trading System Analysis: Using Trading Simulations and Generated Data to Test, Evaluate and Predict Trading System Performance.* New York: McGraw-Hill, 1997.

Very strong on using simulation to develop, test, and evaluate trading strategies.

Bensignor, Rick (Ed.). *New Thinking in Technical Analysis: Trading Models from the Masters.* New York: Bloomberg Press, 2000.

Collection of chapters written by some of the best-known writers in the trading arena; provides numerous excellent ideas for traders.

Blau, W. *Momentum, Direction, and Divergence*. New York: John Wiley & Sons, Inc., 1995.

One of the best books on using momentum for trading.

Chande, Tushar S. & Kroll, Stanley. *The New Technical Trader: Boost Your Profit by Plugging into the Latest Indicators*. New York: John Wiley & Sons, Inc., 1994.

Numerous ideas for applying technical analysis indicators that are rarely discussed in the general trading literature.

Chande, Tushar S. *Beyond Technical Analysis: How to Develop and Implement a Winning Trading System*. New York: John Wiley & Sons, 1997.

Offers many valuable ideas on designing and developing effective trading systems.

Colby, R. W. *The Encyclopedia of Technical Market Indicators*. (2nd Ed.). New York: McGraw-Hill, 2003.

Very comprehensive technical analysis reference book.

Connor, Larry & Alvarez, Cesar. *High Probability ETF Trading: 7 Professional Strategies to Improve Your ETF Trading*. Jersey City, NJ: The Connors Group, 2009.

Valuable book for traders of Exchange Traded Funds (ETFs); there are not a lot of books that focus on ETFs as a trading vehicle.

Deel, Robert. *Trading the Plan: Build Wealth, Manage Money, and Control Risk*. New York: John Wiley & Sons, Inc., 1997.

Informative discussion on the use of leverage in trading.

DiLiddo, Bart. *Stocks, Strategies & Common Sense.* Kanona, NY: HCS Publishing, 1995.

Explains the theoretical underpinnings of the VectorVest approach to stock trading; an essential read for VectorVest users and a valuable book for all investors. Written by the VectorVest Founder and Chairman of the Board.

Dorsey, Thomas J. *Point and Figure Charting: The Essential Application for Forecasting and Tracking Market Prices.* (3rd Ed.). Hoboken, NJ: John Wiley & Sons, Inc., 2007.

One of the best sources of information on the point and figure approach to charting and trading.

Douglas, Mark. *Trading in the Zone: Master the Market with Confidence, Discipline and a Winning Attitude.* New York: New York Institute of Finance, 2009.

Focuses on the important way that a trader's attitudes and perspectives influence his or her trading success or failure.

Droke, Clif. *Moving Averages Simplified.* Columbia, MD: Marketplace Books, 2001.

Good introduction to the theory and application of moving averages as an effective tool in trading.

Elder, Alexander. *Come into My Trading Room: A Complete Guide to Trading.* New York: John Wiley & Sons, Inc., 2002.

3 M's – (Mind, Method, and Money) as a conceptual model for successful trading.

Elder, Alexander. *Entries & Exits: Visits to Sixteen Trading Rooms.* Hoboken, NJ: John Wiley & Sons, Inc., 2006.

Sixteen different approaches to trading; easy to understand and apply.

Elder, Alexander. *Sell and Sell Short.* Hoboken, NJ: John Wiley & Sons, Inc., 2008.

Explains selling short to make money when prices are falling; one of the few books on short selling.

Elder, Alexander. *Study Guide for Trading for a Living: Psychology, Trading Tactics, Money Management.* New York: John Wiley & Sons, Inc., 1993.

Valuable companion to *Trading for a Living*; facilitates understanding concepts and ideas presented in the book.

Elder, Alexander. *Trading for a Living.* New York: John Wiley & Sons, Inc., 1993.

The book I recommend to new traders; provides a wonderful, broad-based introduction to trading.

Harris, Sunny J. *Getting Started in Trading.* New York: John Wiley & Sons, 2001.

Great introduction to trading, written on a very basic level.

Harris, Sunny J. *TradeStation Made Easy: Using Easy Language to Build Profits with the World's Most Popular Software.* Hoboken, NJ: John Wiley & Sons, Inc., 2011.

Excellent book for beginning and advanced traders who want to create and test systems using TradeStation Easy Language programming.

Hirsch, Jeffrey A. & Brown, J. Taylor. *The Almanac Investor: Profit from Market History and Seasonal Trends.* Hoboken, NJ: John Wiley & Sons, Inc., 2006.

Classic book on calendar-based trading.

Hungerford, Larry & Hungerford, Steve. *How to Be a Sector Investor.* New York: McGraw-Hill, 2000.

Good book for traders focusing on trading broad-based business sectors, using Exchange Traded Funds (ETFs) or mutual funds.

Jankovsky, Jason Alan. *Trading Rules That Work: The 28 Essential Lessons Every Trader Must Master.* Hoboken, NJ: John Wiley & Sons, Inc., 2007.

28 rules to guide traders to success.

Kaeppel, Jay. *Seasonal Stock Market Trends: The Definitive Guide to Calendar-Based Stock Market Trading.* Hoboken, NJ: John Wiley & Sons, Inc., 2009.

Detailed descriptions of selected calendar-based market timing approaches and the results of testing these systems. Great book for calendar-based trading.

Katz, Jeffrey Owen & McCormick, Donna L. *The Encyclopedia of Trading Strategies.* New York: McGraw-Hill, 2000.

Wide range of trading topics presented in a disciplined, scientific way; a very valuable addition to a trader's library.

Kaufman, P. J. *Smarter Trading: Improving Performance in Changing Markets.* New York: McGraw-Hill, Inc., 1995.

Many interesting ideas for trading system development; sections on risk control and trading system testing are especially valuable for both new and experienced traders.

LeBeau, C. & Lucas, D. W. *Technical Traders Guide to Computer Analysis of the Futures Market*. New York: McGraw-Hill, 1992.

Great book that describes numerous scientifically sound studies, providing valuable ideas for your own trading system; their discussion of setting and testing stop loss levels is excellent – the best I have ever read.

LeFevre, Edwin. *Reminiscences of a Stock Operator*. Burlington, VT: Fraser Publishing Co., 1980.

A classic book that belongs in any good trading library.

Meyers, T. A. *The Technical Analysis Course: A Winning Program for Investors & Traders*. (3rd Ed.). New York: McGraw-Hill, 2003.

One of the best introductory books on technical analysis.

Murphy, John J. *Technical Analysis of the Financial Markets: A Comprehensive Guide to Trading Methods and Applications*. New York: New York Institute of Finance, 1999.

Considered by many to be the "Bible" of technical analysis; used by the Market Technicians Association as a primary source of information for their Chartered Market Technician (C.M.T.) program.

Nassar, David S. *Rules of the Trade: Indispensable Insights for Online Profits*. New York: McGraw-Hill, 2001.

Numerous rules that can improve a trader's odds of success; a valuable addition to any trader's library.

O'Neil, William J. *How to Make Money in Stocks: A Winning System in Good Times or Bad.* (3rd Ed.), New York: McGraw-Hill, 2002.

Very popular author who developed the well-known CANSLIM approach to stock trading; an easy read and a good addition to a trader's library.

Pardo, Robert. *Design, Testing, and Optimization of Trading Systems.* New York: John Wiley & Sons, Inc., 1992.

Seven-step approach to system design, development, test and evaluation: recommended for traders who want to pursue a logical path to trading success.

Paulos, John Allen. *A Mathematician Plays the Stock Market.* New York: Basic Books, 2003.

Fun to read, especially if you have some interest in the mathematics of trading.

Pruitt, G. & Hill, J. R. *Building Winning Trading Systems with TradeStation.* Hoboken, NJ: John Wiley & Sons, Inc., 2003.

Very good book for traders interested in designing, developing, testing, and evaluating trading systems using the TradeStation software platform.

Schwager, Jack D. *The New Market Wizards: Conversations with America's Top Traders.* New York: John Wiley & Sons, Inc., 1992.

Describes the trading strategies of many well-known traders, providing the reader with numerous good ideas for trading system development.

Sherry, Clifford J. & Sherry, Jason W. *Mathematics of Technical Analysis: Applying Statistics to Trading Stocks, Options, and Futures.* San Jose, CA: to Excel, 2000.

Good book for traders who have a solid background in statistics.

Tharp, Van K. *Trade Your Way to Financial Freedom.* New York: McGraw-Hill, 1999.

Excellent overall book; particularly informative on position-sizing.

Vince, Ralph. *The New Money Management: A Framework for Asset Allocation.* New York: John Wiley & Sons, Inc., 1995.

Contributes many new ideas to the field of money management; reader needs a solid background in mathematics and statistics to take full advantage of the material presented.

Wilder, J. W. Jr. *New Concepts in Technical Trading Systems.* Greensboro, NC: Trend Research, 1978.

Written by a pioneer in technical analysis who developed many popular technical analysis indicators; classic book belongs in every trader's library.

Williams, Larry. *The Secret of Selecting Stocks for Immediate and Substantial Gains.* Brightwaters, NJ: Windsor Books, 1986.

Written by a highly successful and well-known futures trader who applies his expertise to stock trading.

Yahannes, Arefaine G. *The Irwin Guide to Risk & Reward: A Basic Resource for Finance Professionals and Their Clients.* Chicago, IL.: Irwin Professional Publishing, 1996.

Extensive presentation of many risk and reward metrics for various financial investments. A background in mathematics and statistics would be helpful in deriving the most value from this book.

How Would It Work If I Use Your Consulting Services?

I think the easiest way to answer that is to take you through the process, step by step.

I would design, develop, test, and evaluate a complete stock market trading system for you. Your trading system would be custom-designed specifically for you, and would reflect your personal trading style, profit objectives, and risk tolerance.

First Step

We would begin with a telephone interview. During that discussion, I would learn about your trading experience and the type of trading system you want (e.g., aggressive vs. conservative). After our phone call, I begin my research for the best system to meet your personal needs and achieve your goals. My research for your trading system would be conducted in a series of phases.

After I complete the analyses for a research phase, I would send all the results for that phase to you in a spreadsheet. These results would include both the ideas that have produced promising results and those that have not. Then we would have another telephone meeting to discuss the results and answer any questions that you may have.

Planning the Next Steps

Next, I would describe to you my proposed research plan for the following phase. If you have any specific ideas for this next phase, we would discuss those in light of the first phase results. After our telephone discussion, I would begin the work on the next phase. This cycle continues until all the computer simulations have been completed, analyzed, evaluated, and discussed with you.

SYSTEM DELIVERY AND FOLLOW-UP SUPPORT

The final results that I would deliver to you would contain the specific rules for each of the critical components of your total stock market trading system. Those components would have been back tested on historical data and then evaluated on a completely different set of data to provide an unbiased forecast for the likely performance of your system in the future.

Finally, I would make sure that you understand how to implement your trading system rules in making actual stock trades.

CONTACT INFORMATION

If you would like to explore having a custom-designed, total stock trading system developed, tested, and evaluated for performance, please contact me by email and provide a telephone number and a good day and time to reach you.

Email Address: **Consulting@TradeByRules.com**

SOME CLIENT COMMENTS

It can be helpful to know what other people have thought about a product or service that you may be considering getting for yourself. So, I have included some comments made by some of my previous consulting clients.

"In my trading experience, which now exceeds thirty years, I have never found a better teacher than Drew Sands. His intellectual range in regards to trading systems and techniques is encyclopedic, and his knowledge base and expertise is that of a true scientist or statistician. His abilities, therefore, to assess one's trading ideas with reliable research and testing techniques is unmatched anywhere, to include all the big name brokerage houses. With Drew, I feel like I have an entire Wall Street research team to draw upon, and one that puts my interests first. I recommend him as a trading system consultant. If there are any better, I have never found them."

--- Mark Krogness, Washington, DC

"...I wanted to express my appreciation for your great training, advice and help with the analysis strategy that you developed for us. It has proven to be dead-on in accurately diagnosing turns in the market without the normal whipsaws frequently experienced when the market goes through a slow, extended upturn or downturn. ... We feel so fortunate to be catching these turns and we owe so very much of it to you and the things I have learned from you."

--- Roy Jolly, St. George, UT

"...using your services, as a private consultant, has been extremely valuable as an investor to have the personal tools and screening of stocks, customized to fit my trading style, and risk tolerance. I appreciated the time you spent testing these strategies, before presenting them to me, and making sure I had proper money management."

--- Joyce Martinez, San Diego, CA

"Drew Sands was hired as a technical analysis consultant for our private money management firm. He developed a market timing system designed to work with our existing, proprietary stock selection strategy. We have used this market timing system for over three years and are more than pleased as it has provided us with consistent and accurate decisions on when to enter and exit the market."

--- Ken Cornett, Houston, TX

Made in the USA
San Bernardino, CA
24 May 2014